Legal and Regulatory Framework

Legal and Regulatory Framework

For Business in the UK

Sally Ramage Dabydeen

iUniverse, Inc.
New York Lincoln Shanghai

Legal and Regulatory Framework
For Business in the UK

iUniverse, Inc.

For information address:
iUniverse, Inc.
2021 Pine Lake Road, Suite 100
Lincoln, NE 68512
www.iuniverse.com

This book is not intended as a source of advice to any person. The author does not accept any responsibility for anything that any person does or does not do as a result of reading this book.

ISBN: 0-595-32428-2 (pbk)
ISBN: 0-595-66573-X (cloth)

Printed in the United States of America

Contents
outline

PRELIMINARY xiii

CONTRACT LAW 1

EMPLOYMENT LAW 19

BUSINESS STRUCTURES 51

CONSUMER PROTECTION 157

Contents
detailed

PRELIMINARY xiii

    INTERNET SOURCES xiii

CONTRACT LAW 1

    OFFER AND INVITATION TO TREAT 1

        WHAT IS AN OFFER? 1

        QUESTION 1: 2

        ANSWER TO Q1..2

        QUESTION 2 2

        ANSWER TO Q2 2

        QUESTION 3 2

        ANSWER TO Q3 3

        QUESTION 4 4

        ANSWER TO Q4 4

    INTENTION TO CONTRACT 5

    COLLECTIVE AGREEMENTS 8

        QUESTION: 8

    EXPRESS TERMS 9

        1   IMPORTANCE TO THE REPRESENTEE 11

        2   RELATIVE DEGREES OF KNOWLEDGE. 11

    THE NATURE OF CONTRACTUAL TERMS 11

    THE PAROL EVIDENCE RULE 12

        a) RECTIFICATION 13

        b) INVALIDITY 13

        c) NON-OPERATION 13

d) CUSTOM 13

e) INCOMPLETENESS 14

COLLATERAL CONTRACTS 14

CONDITIONS AND GUARANTEES 14

PERFORMANCE AND TERMINATION OF A CONTRACT 15

SUBSTANTIAL PERFORMANCE 15

a) SEVERABLE CONTRACTS 16

b) PREVENTION OF PERFORMANCE 16

c) ACCEPTANCE OF PARTIAL ACCEPTANCE 16

d) SUBSTANTIAL PERFORMANCE 16

TERMINATION OF A CONTRACT 17

EMPLOYMENT LAW 19

STATUTES IN EMPLOYMENT LAW 19

EMPLOYMENT CONTRACT TERMS AND
STATUTORY PROTECTION. 21

THE CONTRACT 21

WRITTEN STATEMENT OF PARTICULARS 22

FAILURE TO GIVE WRITTEN STATEMENT 23

TERMS OF THE CONTRACT 23

EXPRESS AND IMPLIED TERMS 24

COMMON IMPLIED TERMS 24

UNFAIR CONTRACT TERMS ACT1977 25

CHANGES IN TERMS OF CONTRACT 25

EMPLOYMENT CONTRACT TERMS AND
STATUTORY PROTECTIONS 26

QUESTION 1: 26

QUESTION 2 27

QUESTION 3 27

OTHER STATUTORY PROTECTION FOR EMPLOYEES 27

DISCRIMINATIONS 27

EQUAL PAY ACT 1970 28

RACE RELATIONS ACT 1976 28

SOME CASE-LAW SUMMARISED 29
  CONTRACT OF EMPLOYMENT AS OPPOSED TO
  PARTICULARS OF EMPLOYMENT 29
  DUTIES OF THE EMPLOYER 30
  AGE REQUIREMENT—INDIRECT SEX DISCRIMINATION 31
  CASE LAW ON DISABILITY DISCRIMINATION
  AND REASONS FOR DISMISSAL 32
  MISCELLANEOUS 33
  STOP-PRESS 35
MATERNITY AND PARENTAL RIGHTS 36
PARENTAL AND PATERNITY LEAVE 37
PATERNITY LEAVE 37
EQUAL RIGHTS ACT 1996 37
OTHER PROTECTION FOR EMPLOYEES 38
  UK WORK PERMIT CRITERIA AS FROM NOVEMBER 2000 38
OTHER STATUTORY PROTECTION FOR EMPLOYEES 39
  PROBLEM QUESTION: 39
NOTICE, DISMISSAL AND REDUNDANCY 40
  1 TERMINATION BY MUTUAL AGREEMENT 40
  2 TERMINATION BY FRUSTRATION 41
  3 TERMINATION BY EXPIRY 41
  4 DISMISSAL BY THE EMPLOYER 41
  5 TERMINATION BY NOTICE GIVEN BY THE EMPLOYEE 41
  6 TERMINATION BY REPUDIATORY CONDUCT 42
  QUESTION 1 42
  QUESTION 2 43
HEALTH AND SAFETY AT WORK 43
  OCCUPIER'S LIABILITY ACT 1957 44
  HEALTH AND SAFETY AT WORK ACT 1975 44
  THE HEALTH AND SAFETY AT WORK ACT 45
    NEW MAXIMUM PENALTIES FOR HEALTH AND
    SAFETY AT WORK OFFENCES(2003) 45

PERSONAL LIABILITY OF DIRECTORS AND
OTHER COMPANY OFFICERS 47
QUESTION 48
CRIMINALISATION OF EMPLOYERS' CONDUCT 48
HOW DOES THE HUMAN RIGHTS ACT
AFFECT EMPLOYMENT LAW? 49
BUSINESS STRUCTURES 51
PARTNERSHIPS 51
GENERAL PRINCIPLES 51
WHAT IS A PARTNERSHIP? 52
CAPACITY 53
DURATION OF PARTNERSHIP 53
PARTNERSHIP NAME AND PUBLICITY OF INFORMATION 54
AUTOMATICALLY PERMITTED NAMES 54
THE PARTNERSHIP DEED OR AGREEMENT 55
DUTIES OF PARTNERS 58
LIMITED LIABILITY PARTNERSHIPS 58
SPECIMEN PARTNERSHIP DEED 62
CASE-LAW SUMMARIES 76
LEGAL CONTROLS ON PARTNERSHIPS: 76
RESTRAINT OF TRADE CLAUSES: 76
RESTRICTION ON CHOICE OF BUSINESS NAMES 77
GENERAL 77
DISSOLUTION OF PARTNERSHIPS 79
INSOLVENT PARTNERSHIPS 80
PARTNERSHIP ACT 1890 81
LIMITED LIABILITY PARTNERSHIPS ACT 2000 95
COMPANIES 116
INTRODUCTION TO COMPANY LAW 117
LEGAL PERSONALITY 117
CREATION OF CORPORATIONS 118
BY ROYAL CHARTER 118

BY ACT OF PARLIAMENT 118

BY REGISTRATION 118

THE COMPANY'S OWN REGULATION 119

THE GENERAL LAW 120

REGISTRATION 120

COMPANIES LIMITED BY SHARES 120

UNLIMITED COMPANIES 121

PUBLIC COMPANY 121

QUOTED COMPANY 121

CLOSE COMPANIES 121

SMALL AND MEDIUM SIZED COMPANIES 122

PARTNERSHIP COMPANY 122

COMPANY FORMATION 122

STEPS LEADING TO INCORPORATION 122

MEMORANDUM OF ASSOCIATION 123

THE ARTICLES OF ASSOCIATION 125

FORM G10 125

THE CERTIFICATE OF INCORPORATION 126

RIGHTS AND DUTIES 127

DIRECTORS' DUTIES 127

CRIMINALISATION OF EMPLOYERS' CONDUCT 127

CASE LAW 128

BUSINESS NAMES ACT 1985 150

CONSUMER PROTECTION 157

THE BASICS 157

CONTRACTS FOR THE SALE OF GOODS 157

THE SALE OF GOODS ACT 1979 157

THE RIGHT TO SELL THE GOODS 158

DESCRIPTION OF THE GOODS 158

QUALITY AND FITNESS FOR PURPOSE 159

SALE BY SAMPLE 159

OWNERSHIP AND RISK 160

THE RIGHTS OF THE PARTIES 160

CONSUMER CREDIT 161

    A BILL OF EXCHANGE 161

    CHEQUES 162

    CUSTOMERS AND BANKS 162

    DUTIES OWED BY THE BANK 163

    CONSUMER CREDIT AGREEMENT 163

    CREDIT—TOKEN AGREEMENTS 164

    PROTECTION BEFORE YOU MAKE THE AGREEMENT 167

THE CONSUMER PROTECTION ACT 1987 168

THE CONSUMER CREDIT ACT 1974 168

THE TRADE DESCRIPTIONS ACT 1968 169

THE CONSUMER PROTECTION ACT 1987 170

THE UNSOLICITED GOODS AND SERVICES ACT 1971 171

THE DATA PROTECTION ACT 1998 172

NEW DEVELOPMENT ON DATA PROTECTION ACT 172

Preliminary

Internet Sources

http://www.hmso.gov.uk	for statutes
http://www.google.co.uk	search engine
http://www.m25lib.ac.uk/m25/libdata	Institute for Advanced Legal Studies
http://www.tuc.org.uk	TUC
http://www.gftu.org.uk	General Federation of Trade Unions
http://www.cs.ukt.edu	info on sexual harassment
http://www.law-services.org.uk	Law Society
http://www.uklegal.com	legal resources
http://www.lawlounge.com	UK law server
http://www.ndirect.co.uk/~law/bentham.htm	online uk legal materials
http://www.open.gov.uk/oft/ofthome.htm	contract law
http://www.consumerlawpage.com/resource.html	consumer law

CONTRACT LAW

OFFER AND INVITATION TO TREAT

WHAT IS AN OFFER?

An offer is a promise which is capable of acceptance, to be bound on particular terms.

The person who makes the offer is known as the OFFEROR.

The person who receives the offer is called the OFFEREE.

The OFFER sets out the terms on which the offeror is willing to enter into contractual relations with the offeree.

Once an offer is accepted, a contract is established and it becomes binding on the offeror, allowing the offeree to enforce the promise.

The offer must be capable of acceptance and therefore it must not be too vague(fix the terms on which the contract is to be entered).If the offeree REJECTS the offer then that bring it to an end and the offeree cannot subsequently accept it at a later time.

A counter offer brings the original offer to an end also.

But a counter offer is not to be confused with a request for further information. A request for further information does not bring an offer to an end.

Acceptance of an offer creates an enforceable contract. The offeror CAN WITHDRAW his offer at any time before it is accepted but it must be brought to the attention of the offeree. The offeree can be told by a third party, and not necessarily by the offeror himself.

QUESTION 1:

What is an invitation to treat?

ANSWER to Q1

An invitation to treat is NOT an offer.

An invitation to treat is an invitation to others to MAKE OFFERS which the person issuing the invitation to treat may accept or reject as they choose.

The person making the invitation to treat is merely indicating that they are willing to enter into negotiations BUT ARE NOT BOUND to accept any offers made to them.

QUESTION 2

What are examples of invitation to treat?

ANSWER TO Q2

1. The display of goods in a shop window.
2. The display of goods on the shelf of a self-service shop.
3. Advertisements.
4. Tenders where someone wishes a particular work to be done. The person who invites the tender makes an invitation to treat.

QUESTION 3

On Monday, Sarah saw a car in her local garage with a price ticket of £5,000. When she went in to buy it, the garage owner, Mary, laughed and said that the price ticket must have been wrongly marked as the actual price of the car was £9,000. But in the circumstances, she said, she would split the difference (£4,000) and let Sarah have the car for £7,000. Sarah asked for time to think about the offer and Mary said she could have two days. One day later, Sarah found out from her friend Susy that she had bought the car from Mary for £6,000. What are the contractual implications to Mary?

ANSWER to Q3

The original price ticket of £5,000 is merely an invitation to treat. It was not an offer. So Sarah could not insist that Mary sell her the car for £5,000.

It was actually up to Sarah to make an offer for the car.

Mary could have accepted or rejected Sarah's offer.

Mary then offers to sell the car to Sarah for £7,000 which Sarah could have accepted and so forming a BINDING CONTRACT.

Sarah did not accept the offer immediately.

Mary agreed to leave it open for two days.

But a promise to keep an offer open is only binding where there is a SEPARATE CONTRACT to that effect, known as an OPTION CONTRACT in which the offeree/promisee must provide consideration for the promisee to keep the offer open.

But Sarah did not do this.

Any offer can be revoked at any time before acceptance.

For revocation to be effective it must be received by the offeree, though communication of revocation may be made by a reliable third party.

If a reliable third party tells the offeree that the offer is revoked, the revocation is effective and the offeree cannot seek to accept the original offer.

Sarah did not provide any consideration for Mary's promise to keep the offer open for two days.

Therefore it was open to Mary to revoke the offer at any time before Sarah accepted it. Mary revoked the offer to Sarah by selling the car to Susy.

Sarah learnt about Mary's revocation from Susy, a reliable source.

Sarah learnt about the revocation PRIOR to her accepting Mary's offer.

Therefore Sarah HAS NO RIGHTS IN CONTRACT LAW against Mary.

QUESTION 4

Jane's distinctive fibreglass bike is stolen.

She puts an advert in the newspaper.

She offers a reward of £100 to anyone who finds it. Peter finds the bike.

Peter has not seen the advert but his wife has. Peter's wife shows him the advert.

Peter returns the bike to Jane.

Jane refuses to pay the £100 to Peter

Jane says the offer has been withdrawn.

Tell Peter:
1. Is the ad an "offer" or "invitation to treat"?
2. If the ad is an "offer", has Peter accepted?
3. Could Jane argue that her "offer" has been withdrawn before Peter has accepted?
4. Is Peter entitled to the £100?

ANSWER to Q4

1. The advert placed in the newspaper by Jane will almost certainly be regarded as an offer, capable of leading to a contract. Sometimes adverts are merely regarded as invitations to treat but this advert is similar to the advert in Carlill v Carbolic Smoke Ball Co (1893). This is a unilateral contract. Jane's advert is a unilateral contract because only one person is going to be entitled to the reward.

2. Peter has found the bike. But at the time he found the bike he did not know of Jane's advert.

   Can you accept an offer of which you are not aware?

   The most relevant authority is Gibbons v Procter (1891).

   Although Peter does not know of the advert when he found the bike, he did know by the time he returned the bike. If we assume that Jane really wanted her bike returned after it was found, then Peter was acting in response to Jane's advert.

3. In theory, in a unilateral contract, the offeror is entitled to withdraw at any time before performance is complete, the courts, in practice have tended to the view that withdrawal after performance has begun should not be allowed, unless the withdrawal has been communicated.

4. Peter can be advised that he is fully entitled to the £100.

INTENTION TO CONTRACT

You have looked at two elements in a valid contract—offer-and-acceptance and consideration. The third requirement of a valid contract is intention to contract.

Intention to contract is a necessary element in the contractual bond.

Let's look at the situation in which two friends agree to lunch together. John and Jane agree to lunch together. Is this a contract? John promises to pay for the food and Jane promises to pay for the drinks. There is a bargain (agreement plus consideration) but no legal obligations are created. Why? No legal obligations were intended.

Intention to contract is a necessary element in the contractual bond. 'Intention to contract' means the readiness of each party to accept the legal consequences if he does not perform his contract.

In social and domestic agreements, such as between husband and wife, such agreements are most likely to be held to be not contractual. In Balfour v

Balfour (1919) CA, a husband promised to pay his wife £30 a month and when he did not keep the agreement, his wife sued. The Court of Appeal allowed the husband's appeal. Atkin LJ said "…one of the most usual forms of agreement which does not constitute a contract appears to me to be the arrangements which are made between husband and wife…and they are not contracts because the parties did not intend that they should be attended by legal consequences".

The principle in Balfour v Balfour has been applied to an agreement to an agreement between mother and daughter. In this case Jones v Padavatton (1969) CA a mother agreed with her daughter that she would maintain her daughter if the daughter gave up her job to study law. Later, the agreement was varied and the mother agreed to provide a house for her daughter instead of maintenance. On the mother's claim for possession of the house, the Court of Appeal held that the arrangement was not intended to be legally binding and the mother was entitled to possession.

In Parker v Clark (1960) an elderly couple invited their niece and her husband to share their home with them. This involved the younger couple sharing selling their own house. This arrangement was held to be legally binding. Devlin J said that "".the question whether or not there is a binding contract, must, of course, depend on the intention of the parties, to be inferred from the language they use and from the circumstances in which they use it."

In **commercial agreements** there is a presumption that the parties do intend to make a legally enforceable contract. Therefore it is not necessary, in the ordinary run of commercial transactions, for the plaintiff to give affirmative evidence that there was such an intention, although a defendant may defeat this presumption by reference to words used by the parties and/or circumstances in which they used them. See Kleinwort Benson Ltd v Malaysia Mining Corp. (1990) CA.

So we see that in commercial agreements there is a presumed intention to create legal relations. The only exception to this general rule in relation to commercial agreements in the case of ADVERTISING. This exception is to protect advertisers who may in some circumstances be able to rely on an absence of intention to create legal relations in order to avoid being held to the exact words of advertisements

For example, if a beer producer (eg Heinekin) chooses to promote its product by claiming that it refreshes parts which other beers do not reach, it is no doubt seen by reasonable people as a joke and not as a serious claim to be elevated into a contractual promise, although there is the exception in the case of <u>Carlill v Carbolic Smoke Ball Co. (1893) 1QB 256.</u>

In this case, the company had claimed that their product when used properly was an infallible protection against influenza, and had promised to pay £100 to anyone able to show that they had contracted influenza after proper use of a smoke ball. To demonstrate the good faith of this promise the company placed £1000 in a special bank account.

It was particularly in the light of this last fact, that the court was UNWILLING to accept that this promise was no more than overblown advertising and so a claimant w was able to enforce the promise.

The exception depends very much upon the particular facts of the case.

Look at the case of <u>Esso v Customs and Excise [1976] 1 All ER 117.</u>

Esso had organised a promotion in conjunction with the 1970 World Cup. A purchaser of 4 gallons of petrol was entitled to a free 'WORLD CUP COIN'. The VAT man sought to recover tax on the free coins on the ground that they had been produced for general sale.

The case went to the House of Lords. It was decided that there was an intention to create legal relations in respect of the transfer of the coins between garage proprietors and customers purchasing petrol.

Rebutting of the presumption of intention to create legal relations. There are a few cases in which the presumption is rebutted.

<u>Rose and Frank Co v JR Crompton & Bros [1925] AC 445</u>
The plaintiffs were to be the defendants' agents to sell a certain kind of paper in the United States. The document setting out the agency agreement contained a term usually referred to as 'the honourable pledge clause'. It purported to provide that the agreement was to be viewed as a definite expression of intention, but not as a formal or legal agreement subject to the jurisdiction of the courts. The parties continued their relationship for some time, and from time to time the plaintiffs would make a specific order which was met by the defendants.

The defendants then suddenly announced that they would fulfil no more orders, and the plaintiff sued to enforce the general agency agreement.

The House of Lords upheld the 'honourable pledge clause'. They said that in the main agency agreement there was no intention to create legal relations. The presumption of intention was rebutted by the express clause in the agreement

COLLECTIVE AGREEMENTS

It is a common feature of industrial life for trade unions to enter into agreements with employers as to the rates of pay and conditions of work of their members. If the terms of such agreements are then incorporated (as they frequently are) into the individual service contract of each employee with the employer those terms are, of course, legally binding on the parties, ie on the employer and the employee.

But that still leaves the question whether the collective bargain itself is an enforceable contract itself between the trade union and the employer. There is belief among industrialists, trade unionists and lawyers that collective bargains were not enforceable at common law. In the case Ford Motor Co v Amalgamated Union of Engineering (1969), it was held that a collective agreement is not intended to be legally enforceable, and the court will grant no relief for breach of such an agreement. This is an example of 'intention to contract' negatived, not by any actual words used by the parties but by the circumstances surrounding their agreement. The common law position has been substantially affirmed by statute, the Trade Union and Labour Relations Act 1974, which, states in section 18, that a collective agreement is conclusively presumed not to have been intended by the parties to be a legally enforceable contract unless it is in writing and expressly provides that it is so intended.

QUESTION:

Intention to create legal relations:

Roderick and Sally live in a large house and rent out one of the rooms to David.

All three form a group to buy weekly lottery tickets. Roderick usually bought the tickets.

This week one of their tickets won the lottery jackpot of £6 million. Roderick is claiming that, as he bought the tickets, the win is his.

EXPRESS TERMS

A contract contains a number of terms. The terms are, in effect, the obligations of the contract.

If an employer offers an employee a job at £20,000 a year and the employee accepts, one of the TERMS of the contract is that the employer will pay the employee £20,000 a year.

Before they enter into the contract, parties are likely to be involved in negotiations, particularly if it is a complex commercial contract. There is a distinction between TERMS—which do become part of the contract—and REPRESENTATIONS—which do NOT. Representations are statements of fact or opinion. This distinction becomes important where a statement which has been made turns out to be untrue. If such a case went to court, the judge has to decide which statements are CONTRACTUAL TERMS and which are non-contractual REPRESENTATIONS.

Example. I discuss selling my computer with my neighbour. During the discussion, she asks me all about the computer—its age, how much I have used it, whether it has an internet modem, and so on. At the end of these negotiations I agree to sell her my computer for £300. Clearly the contract has more to it than the price. But not all my answers in the discussion will be classified as TERMS OF THE CONTRACT. Some may be and others may be treated as REPRESENTATIONS.

The importance of this distinction between TERMS and REPRESENTATIONS arises where a statement is untrue., ie, where there is a MISREPRESENTATION. If a statement is a TERM of the contract and it is untrue, there is a BREACH OF CONTRACT and the injured party may claim damages amongst other remedies. And even if the misstatement was made entirely innocently, the injured party is entitled to damages. If the misstatement is NOT A TERM of the contract, the injured party will only be entitled to damages in cases of fraud or negligence.

If the misstatement is NOT A TERM of the contract and the misrepresentor acted wholly innocently the injured party will be entitled only to RESCISSION but the court may order damages instead. (more about misrepresentation later).

So it is important to be able to decide whether a statement is a CONTRAC-TUAL TERM or not. This important decision is very difficult. It seems that the basic principle is a question of intention. Did the maker of the statement intend it to be a TERM of the contract? The test of intention is objective. Would a REASONABLE person have taken the statement to be meant as a CONTRACTUAL TERM? This depends on exactly what was said or written and on the circumstances surrounding the transaction.

There are 3 guidelines that show up in case-law:
1. Strength of the statement.
2. Importance of the representee.
3. Relative degree of knowledge.
4. Strength of the statement.

If the person making the statement suggest that the other party check it, the statement will be treated as a term of the contract.

See case-law Ecay v Godfrey (1947).
(The seller of a boat stated that it was sound, but advised the buyer to have it surveyed. This advice showed that the seller did not intend that his statement should be taken as a term of the contract.)

Conversely, if a statement is made in a dogmatic way, so that the other party is dissuaded from checking it, the statement will probable be held to be a con-tractual term. See case-law Schawel v Reade (1913) House of Lords. (The plaintiff was examining a horse with a view to buying it for stud purposes. The defendant said "You need not look for anything: the horse is perfectly sound. If there was anything the matter with the horse I would tell you". The buyer in reliance on this statement bought the horse, which proved to be totally unfit for stud purposes. The case went to the House of Lords. The House of Lords said that the seller's statement was a contractual term.).

1 Importance to the representee

If the representee has made it known that he attaches great importance to a certain fact, and the other party then states that fact to be true, the statement will probably be treated as a CONTRACTUAL TERM. See the case-law Bannerman v White (1861).(An intending buyer of hops asked whether sulphur had been used in their treatment. He added that if it had, he would not even trouble to ask the price. The seller assured him that the hops were not treated with sulphur which was untrue. The court held that the seller's untrue assurance was a TERM of the contract).

2 Relative degrees of knowledge.

If the maker of the statement has some special knowledge or skill compared with the other party, the statement may well be held to be a CONTRACTUAL TERM. If their degrees of knowledge are equal or if the recipient of the statement has the greater knowledge, then the statement may well be held to be a NON-CONTRACTUAL REPRESENTATION. See the case-law Oscar Chess Ltd v Williams (1957) CA. (The defendant traded in his car to Oscar Chess ltd, car dealers. It was a Morris car and the seller described it as a 1948 model. He was given £290 for it. But it turned out to be a 1939 model, worth £175. The statement that the car was a 1948 model was held by the court NOT TO BE A TERM OF THE CONTRACT. The seller was a private individual and who had taken the information honestly from his registration book, which only later turned out to be forge and the buyers were car dealers and so were in as good a position as the seller to know the true age of the car).

THE NATURE OF CONTRACTUAL TERMS

A contract may be made by words or partly by words and partly by conduct. The words may be written or spoken or partly written or partly spoken. The words, whether written or spoken, which the parties use in formulating their agreement, are the express terms of the contract. But those express terms do not always constitute the whole contract; there may be other terms which fail to be implied into it. But for now, let's just look at EXPRESS TERMS.

If a contract is wholly in spoken words, the main task of the judge is to decide what words were used. Where the contract is wholly in writing, there are other problems.

The terms of a contract may be contained in more than one document. If the one document EXPRESSLY REFERS to another document, then that other document, is incorporated into the contract. For example, in a contract for the sale of land, there may be a clause saying "The sale is subject to Clause B of the National Conditions of Sale."

Even if one contractual document does NOT EXPRESSLY REFER to another, it may still be held by the courts that that other document forms part of the contract. See the case-law Edwards v Aberayron Mutual Ship Insurance Society Ltd (1876). In this case it was held that a policy of insurance could be read together with the rules of the mutual insurance society which had issued it, although the policy did not expressly refer to the rules.

THE PAROL EVIDENCE RULE

Where written words have been used and also some spoken words, it is sometimes difficult to decide whether the written words constitute the whole of the contract. This calls for the Parol Evidence Rule to be used. The word "Parol" means any extraneous evidence. So the Parol Evidence Rule meant that such extraneous evidence cannot be admitted to add to, vary or contradict a deed or other written instrument.

Let's look at a case-law., the case of Henderson v Arthur (1907) CA. A covenant in a lease under seal stated that rent must be paid in advance. The lessee was not permitted to give evidence of a previous oral agreement that payment should be made by a bill of exchange maturing in 3 months' time. The two statements were contradictory. It was held that it was common sense to prefer the written expression of intent. But the Rule does not prevent the courts from resorting to extrinsic evidence where such evidence is consistent with the intention of the parties.

Also, there are EXCEPTIONS to the Parol Evidence Rule. The exceptions are

a) Rectification

b) Rectification Invalidity

c) Rectification Non-operation

d) Rectification Custom

e) Rectification Incompleteness

a) Rectification

If the plaintiff argues that the meaning of the contract is X and that X was orally expressed between the parties BEFORE the contract was put in writing and that if X is not the meaning of the contract, its wording should be changed to bring it in line with the meaning X. On the rectification point, the Parol Evidence Rule DOES NOT APPLY as the point depends entirely on the extrinsic evidence.

Justification is an equitable remedy, which is available only at the discretion of the court.

b) Invalidity

The Parol Evidence Rule excludes extrinsic evidence of the contents of a contract but not extrinsic evidence relating to its validity. Evidence of matters outside the writing can be given to show some invalidating cause such as misrepresentation, mistake, incapacity, or absence of consideration.

c) Non-operation

The Parol Evidence Rule does not PREVENT evidence being given to prove that the contract does not YET operate or has ceased to operate. In the case Pym v Campbell (1865) the parties entered into a written agreement for the sale of an invention. When the plaintiff sued for breach of this agreement the defendants were permitted to give evidence of an oral agreement that the written agreement was not to operate until a third party had approved the invention and that the third party had never approved it.

d) Custom

The Parol Evidence Rule does not forbid extrinsic evidence of custom. In Hutton v Warren (1836) a plaintiff tenant, who had been given notice to vacate a farm, was permitted to give evidence of a local custom entitling him to a fair allowance for seeds and labour.

e) Incompleteness

The most important limitation of the Parol Evidence Rule is that it DOES NOT APPLY WHERE THE WRITTEN AGREEMENT IS NOT THE WHOLE AGREEMENT. So it applies if the written agreement is the whole agreement.

COLLATERAL CONTRACTS

Sometimes the courts call a statement which is not a term of the main contract and is not a mere representation a "collateral contract". This is because it is a TERM of another contract, standing side by side with the main contract. An example of a collateral contract is found in the case De Lasalle v Guildford.

The defendant was negotiating to let his house to the plaintiff. The plaintiff refused to hand over his signed part of the lease unless he was assured that the drains were in order. The defendant gave him this assurance. The drains were not in order and the plaintiff sued for damages and succeeded on the footing that there had been a BREACH, not of the tenancy contract but of the COLLATERAL(DRAINS) CONTRACT. This collateral contract must also have all the necessary elements of a valid contract—agreement, consideration and an intention to be legally bound. The consideration must be separate from the consideration of the main contract. case mentioned, it was not possible to say whether the rent was consideration for the promise about the drains as well as fulfilling the main contract, but consideration for the drains promise was the IMPLIED promise to enter the main contract, ie. "If you promise that the drains are in order I will execute the lease"

CONDITIONS AND GUARANTEES

If a contract contains more than one TERM, as it usually does, it may well be that the TERMS ARE NOT OF EQUAL IMPORTANCE. The more important terms are referred to as CONDITIONS and the less important as WARRANTIES.

Breach of the terms of a contract gives the victim the right to treat the contract as repudiated. Breach of warranty, on the other hand, does NOT entitle the victim to treat the contract as repudiated but only entitles the victim to claim damages. These words, condition and warranty come from usage in the Sale of Goods Act 1893 but are now widely used in contract law.

PERFORMANCE AND TERMINATION OF A CONTRACT

We are going to consider the 4 ways in which a contract may come to an end:

a) Performance

b) Agreement

c) Frustration

d) Breach

Then we will consider remedies.

The most obvious way in which a contract may come to an end is by its being performed.

If X and Y make a contract under which X is to perform some service and Y is to pay him for it, then when X performs his service and Y pays him for it, both parties have discharged their contractual obligations and the contract is at an end.

Generally, performance must exactly match what the parties agreed to do. If he does something less than or different from what he agreed to do, he has not discharged his contractual obligation and so as a result, he is not entitled to payment.

SUBSTANTIAL PERFORMANCE

He cannot sue on the contract because his own complete performance is a CONDITION PRECEDENT to his right to sue.

This is the general RULE but there are 4 EXCEPTIONS. These exceptions are as important as the general rule. The exceptions are:

a) Severable contracts

b) Prevention of performance

c) Acceptance of partial performance

d) Substantial performance

a) Severable contracts

Some contracts are severable. It depends upon the intention of the parties, which has to be determined by considering the express and implied terms of the contract.

An example of a SEVERABLE CONTRACT is found in the case <u>Ritchie v Atkinson (1808)</u>. A ship-owner agreed to carry a cargo of hemp, freight to be £5 a ton. He in fact only took part of the cargo. The court decided that he could recover freight proportional to the quantity carried. It is the particular OBLIGATION within a contract that is entire or severable. So the obligation to carry to a particular destination is entire. The obligation to carry a particular quantity is severable.

b) Prevention of performance

If a party to a contract performs part of the work that he has undertaken, and is then prevented by the fault of the other party from finishing the work, he can sue. He can sue whether the contract is entire or severable. He can sue either for damages or breach of contract. Or he can sue for QUANTUM MERUIT and so get a reasonable remuneration for the work he has done.

An example is the case <u>Planche v Colburn</u>. The plaintiff agreed to write a book on costume and ancient armour, to be published by the defendants in a series called "The juvenile library". He was to be paid £X on completion of the book. The defendants then abandoned the series. On a QUANTUM MERUIT claim he was awarded £½ X.

c) Acceptance of partial acceptance

If one party partially performs his obligation and the other party accepts the work, it may be possible to infer that the parties have agreed to abandon the original contract (whether severable or entire) and to make a new contract, under which the party making partial performance is entitled to a reasonable remuneration.

d) Substantial performance

A party who performs his obligations defectively, but substantially, can enforce the contract. But there are limits to the doctrine of substantial performance, as illustrated in the case law <u>Bolton v Mahadeva (1972) CA</u>. In this case the plaintiff had contracted to install central heating in the defendant's house for £560. At the trial it was proved that the house was 10% less warm than it should have been and that because of a defective flue there were fumes in the living rooms. It would have cost £174 to put this right. The Court of Appeal held that the plaintiff was not able to rely on the doctrine of substantial performance. So the plaintiff got nothing.

Where a party performs only partially or defectively, although he may be able to sue on the contract, he is not entirely discharged. If the incompleteness or defectiveness of his performance amounts to a breach of contract, he can be sued for that breach.

The case we looked at as an example of severable contracts, <u>Ritchie v Atkinson</u> had another face to it. Because although Ritchie won his action for proportional freight, he was later held liable in damages for failing to carry the rest of the cargo. (the case of <u>Atkinson v Ritchie (1809)</u>.

We have now covered the four exceptions to performance.

TERMINATION OF A CONTRACT

A contract is discharged on performance. It comes to an end. It can also be terminated after damages are paid for loss. In this case it is discharged by frustration. A contract can also be discharged by breach of contract in which a secondary obligation to pay damages for loss caused continues.

These discharges are to VALID CONTRACTS.

An INVALID CONTRACT can also be terminated. A contract may be INVALID because it is affected by MISTAKE, by MISREPRESENTATION, by INCAPACITY, by DURESS, by UNDUE INFLUENCE or by ILLEGALITY. In many circumstances no legal process is necessary to effect the termination of an invalid contract. A void contract gives rise to NO OBLIGATION TO PERFORM. So the party that asserts its invalidity need do nothing and can plead the invalidity as an action for breach. In the case where there is misrepresentation in the contract, that contract is voidable but that contract remains valid until it is brought to an end by the party empowered by law to do so. This process of termination is known as "rescission".

EMPLOYMENT LAW

STATUTES IN EMPLOYMENT LAW

Apportionment Act 1870

Equal Pay Act 1970

European Communities Act 1972

Employment Agencies Act 1973

Health and Safety at Work Act 1974

Rehabilitation of Offenders Act 1974

Sex Discrimination Act 1974

Race Relations Act 1976

Patents Act 1977

Unfair Contract Terms Act 1977

State Immunity Act 1978

Employment Protection Act 1978

Employment Act 1980

Social Security and Housing Benefits Act 1982

Employment Act 1982

Data Protection Act 1984

Companies Act 1985

Insolvency Act 1986

Wages Act 1986

Sex Discrimination Act 1986

Public Order Act 1986

Income and Corporation Taxes Act 1988

Employment Act 1988

Access to Medical reports Act 1988

Education Reform Act 1988

Social Security Act 1989

Employment Act 1989

Contracts (Applicable Law) Act 1990

Employment Act 1990

Offshore Safety Act 1992

Trade Union and Labour Relations Act 1992

Trade Union Reform and Employment Rights Act 1993

Pensions Schemes Act 1993

Insolvency Act 1994

Deregulation and Contracting Out Act 1994

Pensions Act 1995

Disability Discrimination Act 1995

Employment Tribunals Act 1995

Employment Rights Act 1996

Armed Forces Act 1996

Asylum and Immigration Act 1996

Police (Health and Safety) Act 1997

Employment Rights (Dispute Resolution)Act 1997

Public Interest Disclosure Act 1998

Data Protection Act 1998

National Minimum Wages Act 1998

Human Rights Act 1998

Tax Credits Act 1999

Disability Rights Commission Act 1999

Employment Relations Act 1999

Welfare Reform and Pensions Act 1999

Contracts Act 1999

Regulation and Investigatory Powers Act 2000

Tax Credits Act 2002

Employment Act 2002

EMPLOYMENT CONTRACT TERMS AND STATUTORY PROTECTION.

The contract between an employer and an employee is usually referred to as a contract of employment or a contract of service.

There are 3 issues in connection with a contract of employment.

1. Is the particular agreement under which a person works a 'contract of employment' or is that person 'self-employed'?
2. The TERMS of the particular contract of employment.
3. Remedies available for breach of the contract of employment.

An employer may engage or refuse to engage any person, subject to the statutory provisions relating to children and young persons, discrimination on grounds of race or disability or trade union membership and the provisions relating to the employment of foreign nationals.

THE CONTRACT

A contract of employment may be either written or oral, or a mixture of the two. So it can be a document drawn up by solicitors and signed by both parties or the contract can be just a chat over a cup of tea. Usually, executives and other senior people are employed using written agreements drafted by solicitors. These agreements are often for a fixed term. For example, a director cannot be employed for with a five year agreement because this would be a void contract under the Companies Act 1985, section 319. Such written agreements usually contain restrictive covenants (such as RESTRAINT OF TRADE, CONFIDENTIALITY AND EMPLOYEE INVENTIONS).

Less senior employees may be asked to sign a standard form of contract of employment.
In other cases, the contract will be contained in an exchange of letters, or terms may be agreed orally at an interview.

Provided that the parties are in agreement over the essential terms of the contract, such as hours and wages, there will be a valid contract of employment enforceable by either party.

WRITTEN STATEMENT OF PARTICULARS

Although the law does not require the contract itself to be in writing, every employer is required to give each employee a written statement of particulars of CERTAIN TERMS OF HIS CONTRACT NOT LATER THAN TWO MONTHS AFTER the beginning of the employee's employment. (Employment Rights Act 1996, section 1).

If employment ends within the 2 month period, a statement must still be given (ERA 1996 section 2(6)) unless the employment continued for less than one month. (Employment Rights Act 1996, section 198).

The Employment Act 2002 made amendments to the Employment Rights Act 1996 to permit the use of documents as an alternative to a Statement of particulars.

The WRITTEN STATEMENT MUST CONTAIN:

1. Name of the employer and the employee
2. Date the employment began
3. Date of start of CONTINUOUS employment
4. Scale or rate of remuneration
5. The intervals at which remuneration is paid (weekly or monthly)
6. Terms and conditions relating to hours of work (eg normal working hours)
7. Terms and conditions relating to entitlement to holidays including public holidays and holiday pay, incapacity for work due to sickness or injury, pension and pension schemes
8. The length of notice which the employee is obliged to give and entitled to receive to terminate his contract of employment
9. The title of the job and a brief description of the work for which he is employed
10. Whether this is intended to be permanent employment, or if fixed term, the date when it is to end
11. Either the place of work or where the employee is required to work at various places, those addresses and the employer's address

12. Any collective agreements which directly affect the terms and conditions of the employment, including the persons by whom they were made where the employer is not a party and

13. Where the employee is required to work outside the UK for more than 1 month, certain particulars concerning that period, the currency of remuneration,

14. additional remuneration and benefits and any terms and conditions relating to his return to the UK.

As an alternative to setting out all these particulars in the written statement, the Employment Rights Act 1996 section 2(2), (3) that the written statement can just refer to some other document which the employee will have access to, and ay just refer the employee to the law or to a collective agreement which directly affects his terms and conditions.

If there are any changes to this written statement, the employer must do so in writing.

FAILURE TO GIVE WRITTEN STATEMENT

An employee who has not been provided with the particulars as specified in the Employment Act 2002 may make a complaint relating to the failure to an employment tribunal (ERA 1996 section 11(1)).

TERMS OF THE CONTRACT

The parties are free to agree any terms they wish, subject to certain limitations. For example, that the words used must be interpreted in the context which existed and was known to both parties at the time when the contract was made. Obviously, the terms cannot be illegal as this would void the contract. If a contract term is unlawful (eg to do an unlawful act) or contrary to public policy (eg a contract for immoral purposes) it will be unenforceable in a court of law. For example, contracts which are a fraud on the Inland Revenue cannot be relied upon to pursue claims for wrongful or unfair dismissal. A foreign employee knowingly working illegally without a work permit will not be able to complain of unfair dismissal. And ignorance of the law as opposed to the facts is no excuse. But the distinction between lawful tax avoidance and unlawful tax evasion must be remembered. An employee can lawfully arrange matters so as to minimise tax liability and this does not make his contract of employment illegal (<u>Lightfoot v D & J Sports Ltd [1996] IRLR 64</u>).

The fact that a contract is unenforceable by reason of illegality does not preclude a person employed under such a contract from bringing claims of SEX DISCRIMINATION OR RACE DISCRIMINATION OR DISABILITY DISCRIMINATION. The reason for this is that such actions do not seek to enforce the unenforceable contract. <u>Leighton, Michael & Charalambous [1996] IRLR 67</u>) unless the claim arises because of their conduct. Also, if an employer stipulates an unlawful term in the sense that if it were carried out the employer would be liable to criminal prosecution or a civil action, this term would be unenforceable by him.

An employer or employee may not contract out of these ACTS:

- Sex Discrimination Act 1975 (section 77)
- Equal Pay Act 1970
- Race Relations Act 1976 (section 72)
- Trade Union and Labour Relations (Consolidation) Act 1992 (section 288)
- Disability Discrimination Act 1995 (section 9)
- Working Time Regulations 1998
- Employment act 2002 (section 30(2))

EXPRESS AND IMPLIED TERMS

The terms of the contract may be EXPRESS or IMPLIED or INCORPORATED.
EXPRESS TERMS are those that the parties specifically deal with and agree upon. The express terms will be found in the contract of employment. The provisions set out in a STATEMENT OF WRITTEN PARTICULARS will be evidence of the express terms but the statement of written particulars is not the contract itself.

COMMON IMPLIED TERMS

Many terms of the contract will not be specifically set out or stated. There may be many rights or obligations on either side which are left unexpressed and unspecified. The general rule is that a term may be implied into a contract if it is necessary to give it business efficacy. Terms may be implied if they are customary in the trade or if they form the usual practice of the employer if it is sufficiently well known.

Terms commonly implied are the employee's duties of:

1. Fidelity
2. Obedience
3. Working with due diligence and care
4. Not using or disclosing the employer's trade secret or confidential information.

Terms commonly implied as the employer's duties of not destroying the relationship of trust and confidence between the employer and the employee and to take care of the employee's health and safety.

Both parties have the commonly implied duty to give a reasonable period of notice of termination where no specific notice has been agreed.

UNFAIR CONTRACT TERMS ACT1977

Neither a contract term nor a notice may validly exclude or restrict liability for death or personal injury resulting from negligence (UCTA 1977 section 2(1)). In the case of Johnstone v Bloomsbury Health Authority [1991] ICR 269, the Court of Appeal considered that this provision would prevent the health authority from relying on an EXPRESS TERM in a junior hospital doctor's contract of employment under which he could be required to work up to 88 hours a week. So the UCTA applied to contracts of employment.

CHANGES IN TERMS OF CONTRACT

No change in the terms of an employee's contract may be made without his consent. Such consent may be EXPRESS by the employee agreeing to the change orally or in writing. Or it may be implied by the employee continuing to work for the employer without protest for a significant period of time whilst being aware of the change.

If the change in contractual terms is of great importance to the employer and the employee does not agree, the employer can give notice to terminate the original contract and offer new terms. This takes great care as it can lead to the employee bringing a claim for unfair dismissal.

Any change in terms to which the employee does not consent is a breach of contract If the change is a significant one, the employee may be entitled to resign and allege that he has been constructively dismissed. However where an employer unilaterally imposes radically different terms of employment, it may be interpreted that the employer has terminated the original contract and replaced it with another. This would mean that the employer dismissed the employee and immediately re-employed the employee and this would entitle the employee to bring unfair dismissal proceedings. (Alcan Extrusions v Yates [1996] IRLR 327)

EMPLOYMENT CONTRACT TERMS AND STATUTORY PROTECTIONS

QUESTION 1:

Production workers for TOTALITY Limited have received a Christmas bonus every year for the past ten years. During that time, the company has always traded at a profit but, last year, the company traded at a loss and no bonus was paid.

Last week, the company issued a new rule which was posted on the notice board. The rule states that management reserves the right to require any employee to submit to a body search upon leaving the company premises, in order to check that property of the company is not being removed.

All the terms and conditions of employment of production workers working for the company are the product of a collective agreement negotiated between their union and the company, although the agreement has now terminated.

One of the clauses in the agreement stated that redundancy selection would be on the basis of LIFO (LAST IN FIRST OUT). The company now wishes to make 5 production workers redundant on the basis of "lack of management potential".

WHAT ARE THE CONTRACTUAL IMPLICATIONS OF THESE CHANGES?

QUESTION 2

"What are the consequences of deciding that a person is an employee?"

QUESTION 3

"Do collective agreements have a major impact on employees' terms and conditions?

OTHER STATUTORY PROTECTION FOR EMPLOYEES

The topics we shall cover are

- Sex Discrimination Act 1975
- Race Relations Act 1976
- Disability Discrimination Act 1995
- Employment Equality Regulations 2003
- Disability Discrimination
- Health and Safety at Work
- Equal Pay Act 1970
- Unfair Dismissal (as part of the Employment Rights Act 1996)

Discriminations

Sex, race, religion and disability discrimination matter when employers advertise for prospective employees.

An employer may use any interviewing and selection procedures he wishes, providing they are not discriminatory within the meaning of the above Acts. And in arranging an interview for a disabled person, it may be necessary for the employer to make reasonable adjustments to enable that person to attend.

An employer is free to select whomsoever he chooses subject to the following:

1. The restriction on the employment of children and young persons.

2. The restriction on the employment of foreign employees.

3. The restriction of excluding a person from any office, profession or occupation or employment by reason of a spent conviction.

4. The bar on refusing a person employment because he is or is not a trade union member.

Equal Pay Act 1970

The Equal Pay Act 1970 enables women to claim equal pay with men. A woman is regarded as employed on like work with men if, but only if, her work and theirs is of the same or of a broadly similar nature and the difference (if any) between the things she does and the things they do are not of practical importance in relation to the performance of her contract of employment.

Race Relations Act 1976

The RRA 1976 is concerned with 4 different types of discrimination:

1. Direct discrimination

2. Indirect discrimination

3. Victimisation and

4. Harassment

1   **Direct discrimination** occurs where an employer treats an employee less favourably on racial grounds.

2   **Indirect discrimination** occurs when the employer requires its employees to comply with an apparently race-neutral condition of requirement that, in practice, is more difficult for members of a particular race to comply with.

3   **Victimisation** occurs where an employer treats an employee less favourably by reason that the employee has performed one of a number of acts which the RRA 1976 identifies as triggering a need for protection.

4   **Harassment** occurs where an employer violates an employee's dignity or creates an intimidatory, hostile, degrading, humiliating or offensive working environment.

SOME CASE-LAW SUMMARISED

Contract of Employment as opposed to Particulars of Employment

Whether the contract is written, partly written or just oral, the employee who has a working week of 8 hours or more, has a right, under the Employment Rights Act 1996, to receive a written statement of particulars of employment.

The idea behind these requirements is simply to let the employee know where he stands.

The written statement of particulars is NOT the contract of employment. This is a very important point. There was a case where an employee treated his written statement of particulars for employment as his contract of employment and took the employer to an employment appeal tribunal hearing on it. The case is <u>System Floors (UK) Ltd v Daniel [1981] IRLR 475.</u> The tribunal said

"The statement of particulars provides a very strong prima facie evidence of what were the terms of the contract between the parties. Nor is the statement of the terms finally conclusive ; at most it places a heavy burden on the employer to show that the actual terms of contract are different from those which the employer has set out in the statutory statement (particulars)"

So, if an employee gets a written contract, it would contain all the details in the written statement of particulars which the employer had to give the employee by law (ERA 1996 s1) and also such things, not prescribed by law, as

- lay-offs
- guaranteed weeks
- pension schemes
- holidays.

These other things are to be agreed between the two parties.

The law does not dictate things such as time or money (apart from complying with the Minimum Wages Act) The CONTRACT will also contain **implied terms.**

For example, in the case-law <u>Stevenson v Teeside Bridge and Engineering [1971] 1 All ER 296,</u> a construction engineer's contract contained an implied term that he would move his place of work as each job was completed.

On the other hand, if such a term is not implied, the employer can end up in breach of contract, as in the case-law <u>Cox v Phillips Industries Ltd [1976] 2 All ER 161</u>. In this case Mr Cox was moved from one job to another by his employer. This made him depressed and he became ill and left his employment and then sued his employer for breach of contract. He won damages of £500.

Duties of the employer

He must comply with the statutes

- Sex Discrimination Act
- Race Relations Act
- Disability Discrimination Act

In <u>Greig v Community Industry and Ahern [1979] IRLR 158,</u> Miss Greig accepted employment as a painter and decorator. On her first day, the personnel officer refused to let her start work because she was the only female in the gang, had he let her join the gang. He offered her other work instead. She refused. She left and took the firm to tribunal and won the sex discrimination case.

In the case <u>Hussein v Saintes Complete House Furnishers [1979] IRLR 337</u>, the employers had advertised for a sales assistant who must live MORE THAN 5 miles of Liverpool City centre. Mr Hussein took Saintes to court on race discrimination because most coloured people lived within this 5 mile limit and mostly white people could afford to live outside the 5 mile criteria. He won. It was unlawful indirect race discrimination.

Age requirement—indirect sex discrimination

Price v Civil Service Commission [1978] IRLR 3
In this case the Civil Service advertised that the requirement was that applicants had to be aged between 17 and 28 years. This was unlawful indirect discrimination because there are more men than women available for work between these ages, due to the fact of child-bearing and child rearing.?????
Another similar decision:

Home Office v Holmes [1984] IRLR 299
Requirement for "full-time" working was held to be indirect sex discrimination.

Wright v Rugby Borough Council [1984] The Times, 29.10.84
The application form said that the requirement was for "set hours, eg 9 am–pm)
Indirect sex discrimination.

Madla (Sewa Singh) v Dowell Lee [1983] ICR 385
The House of Lords said that "…ethnic origins, in the definition of racial group, meant a group which was a segment of the population distinguished from others by a sufficient combination of shared customs, beliefs, traditions and characteristics derived from a common or presumed common past, even if not drawn from what in biological terms was a common racial stock.". They said that Sikhs were a racial group entitled to the protection of the RRA 1976.

Seide v Gillette Industries Ltd [1980] IRLR 427
Jews are members of a racial group.

Commission for Racial Equality v Dutton [1989] IRLR 8
Gypsies are members of a racial group in the sense that they belong to the Romany race. BUT mere habitual wanderers are NOT.

Crown Suppliers (PSA) v Dawkins [1993] ICR 517
Rastafarians ARE NOT an ethnic group for the purposes of the RRA 1976.

Northern Joint Police Board v Power [1997] IRLR 610
The English are a separate racial group under RRA 1976.

BBC Scotland v Souster [2001] IRLR 150
The Scots are a separate racial group for purposes of the RRA 1976

Kebir v Bangladesh Women's Association (unreported, 10026/92)
The Sylhesis from Sylhet in Bangladesh do NOT constitute a racial group.
They are only from a particular region of India.

Section 3(1) RRA 1976 provides that "racial group" can be defined by
COLOUR ie that a racial group, eg. black people, may be of more than one ethnic origin.

Cardiff Women's Aid v Hartup [1994] IRLR 390
A charity advertised for a "black or Asian woman". Mrs Hartup, who was white,
brought proceedings in the employment tribunal alleging that the effect of the
advertisement was that she had been discriminated against in the arrangements made for the purpose of determining who should be offered employment. This was contrary to RRA 1976, section 4(1). But because she HAD
NOT applied for the post, but only saw the advertisement, the tribunal found
that the advert had INTENTION to discriminate but Mrs Hartup COULD
NOT CLAIM to have suffered any actual discrimination.

Ojutiku v Manpower Services Commission [1982] ICR 661
Access to training case. Employer cannot deliberately omit or refuse training of
employees on racial grounds. RRA 1976, section 4(2)(a).

Derby Specialist Fabrication Ltd v Burton [2001] IRLR 69
Employer cannot dismiss employee on racial grounds. (under unfair dis-
missal)
Race Discrimination Act 1976 (Amendment) Regulations 2003 (Statutory
Instrument 2003/1626) and RRA 1976, section 4(4A).

Case law on disability discrimination and reasons for dismissal

A recent case Hutchinson 3G UK Limited v Mason (unreported December
2003) shows the importance of being up-front about the reasons for dismissal,
especially where ill health is concerned. The employee had been off sick for
some time before he revealed to his employer the true extent of his ill health—

namely his cocaine addiction and clinical depression. The employer dismissed him on medical grounds, without specifying reasons.

He brought an unfair dismissal case against the employer in which the employer claimed that the employee had been dismissed for dishonesty (because he had misled them about the nature of his illness). However the Employment Tribunal did not believe the employer and decided that the real reason for the dismissal was absence from work rather than dishonesty. In fact, the unfair dismissal claim ultimately succeeded on the basis that the employer had adopted an unfair procedure.

In addition, even though drug addiction is specifically excluded from being a disability, the employee was able to bring a claim of disability discrimination because his depressive disorder—which is a disability under the Disability Discrimination Act—had contributed to his absence from work to such an extent that the tribunal was able to say that the dismissal was because of it.

The employer was unable to show that it had considered reasonable adjustments—such as a phased return to work—and, consequently, the claim for disability discrimination succeeded.

The unfortunate result for the employer, in trying to act in the best interests of the employee and being discreet about the real reason for dismissal, was that not only did it make it almost inevitable that the dismissal would be unfair (because the wrong reason was given) but it also meant that it could not take advantage of a potentially good justification for the discrimination (the employee's dishonesty)

Miscellaneous

Contract of Employment as opposed to Particulars of Employment
Whether the contract is written, partly written or just oral, the employee who has a working week of 8 hours or more, has a right, under the Employment Rights Act 1996, to receive a written statement of particulars of employment.
The idea behind these requirements is simply to let the employee know where he stands.
The written statement of particulars is NOT the contract of employment. This is a very important point. There was a case where an employee treated his written statement of particulars for employment as his contract of employment

and took the employer to an employment appeal tribunal hearing on it. The case is *System Floors (UK) Ltd v Daniel [1981] IRLR 475.* The tribunal said:

> "The statement of particulars provides a very strong prima facie evidence of what were the terms of the contract between the parties. Nor is the statement of the terms finally conclusive ; at most it places a heavy burden on the employer to show that the actual terms of contract are different from those which the employer has set out in the statutory statement (particulars)"

So, if an employee gets a written contract, it would contain all the details in the written statement of particulars which the employer had to give the employee by law (ERA 1996 s1) and also such things, not prescribed by law, as
lay-offs
guaranteed weeks
pension schemes
holidays.
These other things are to be agreed between the two parties.
The law does not dictate things such as time or money (apart from complying with the Minimum Wages Act) The CONTRACT will also contain **implied terms.**

For example, in the case-law *Stevenson v Teeside Bridge and Engineering [1971] 1 All ER 296,* a construction engineer's contract contained an implied term that he would move his place of work as each job was completed.

On the other hand, if such a term is not implied, the employer can end up in breach of contract, as in the case-law *Cox v Phillips Industries Ltd [1976] 2 All ER 161*. In this case Mr Cox was moved from one job to another by his employer. This made him depressed and he became ill and left his employment and then sued his employer for breach of contract. He won damages of £500.

DUTIES OF THE EMPLOYER
He must comply with the statutes
Sex Discrimination Act
Race Relations Act
Disability Discrimination Act

In *Greig v Community Industry and Ahern [1979] IRLR 158,* Miss Greig accepted employment as a painter and decorator. On her first day, the personnell officer refused to let her start work because she was the only female in the gang, had he let her join the gang. He offered her other work instead. She refused. She left and took the firm to tribunal and won the sex discrimination case.

In the case *Hussein v Saintes Complete House Furnishers [1979] IRLR 337*, the employers had advertised for a sales assistant who must live MORE THAN 5 miles of Liverpool City centre. Mr Hussein took Saintes to court on race discrimination because most coloured people lived within this 5 mile limit and mostly white people could afford to live outside the 5 mile criteria. He won. It was unlawful indirect race discrimination.

Stop-press

"SCATTER-GUN" WORKPLACE CLAIMS RISE

Article in the Times Newspaper, Business Section, February 26th, 2004. by Elizabeth Judge.

Employers are being forced into large out-of-court settlements by litigious staff who are adopting a "scattergun" approach to tribunal cases, lawyers say.

Employees, many spurred on by "no-win, no-fee" lawyers, are being encouraged to bundle together four or five claims at once.

Many have weak cases, but hope that by confronting their small employer with a package of claims they will strike fear into him and force a settlement, rather than defending several claims.

The trend has been spotted by employment experts who have studied tribunal statistics. While the number of tribunal claims has gone down in the past two years—applications to tribunals last year fell from 128,000 to 105,000—the complicity of the claims (the number of claims bundled together) has risen dramatically. The statistics for last year, due out from the Office of the Tribunals within weeks, are expected to show a continued increase in the number of "composite" claims, lawyers say.

James Davies, employment expert at Lewis Silkin, the law firm, says "Claims are becoming increasingly complicated and it is very difficult for the small employer particularly."

Many businesses, Mr Davies says, settle not only because of the fears of costs they could incur, but also because of concerns for their reputation. "They know that if it gets out that they are facing a claim for something like sex discrimination, for example, they run the risk of completely damaging their company."

Lawyers say that more workers are attempting to intimidate employers into pay-outs. But the increase in litigation, they say, is also because of the burgeoning number of grounds on which employees can sue.

> "Before they have even been recruited, employees now have five grounds—including sex and racial discrimination—on which they can bring a claim"

MATERNITY AND PARENTAL RIGHTS

The Employment Protection Act 1975 created statutory rights for women employees.

At present, women employees who can satisfy the relevant qualifying conditions have the following statutory rights:

1. Paid time-off to receive ante-natal care.

2. 26 weeks maternity leave.

3. Protection from detriment by reason of pregnancy, childbirth or maternity.

4. Maternity pay.

5. Return to work after ordinary maternity leave or additional maternity leave (a further 26 weeks).

6. Offer of alternative work before being suspended on maternity grounds.

7. Remuneration on suspension on maternity grounds.

PARENTAL AND PATERNITY LEAVE

Since 15th December 1999, there is the Maternity and Parental Leave Regulations 1999, Statutory Instrument 2001/4041.

The right to parental leave is exercisable by any employee with one year's continuous service who has, or expects to have, responsibility for a child. This means 'parental responsibility' or registration as the child's father.

The period of parental leave is set at 13 weeks for each child. Parents of disabled children may take up to 18 weeks leave. Ordinarily the entitlement must be exercised before the child's 5th birthday, except for parents of disabled children, where parental leave can be taken until the child's 18th birthday.

PATERNITY LEAVE

The Employment Act 2002 introduced an entitlement to paternity leave., available both on the birth and adoption of a child.

The employee may take either one week's leave, or two weeks consecutive leave.

EQUAL RIGHTS ACT 1996

The Equal Rights Act 1996 section 98 states that once the fact of dismissal has been established, it is for the employer to show:

a) what was the reason for the dismissal and

b) that it was for one of the following acceptable reasons:

1. Reasons related to the capacity or qualifications of the employee for performing work of the kind which he was employed to do.

2. Reasons related to the conduct of the employee.

3. That the employee was redundant.

4. That the employee could not continue to work in the position which he held without contravention., OR

5. Some other substantial reason of a kind such as to justify the dismissal of an employee holding the position which that employee held.

Other notes

When employing foreign nationals, the employer must abide with the United Kingdom's Work Permit criteria. (handout)

OTHER PROTECTION FOR EMPLOYEES

UK WORK PERMIT CRITERIA as from November 2000

The Government has lowered the skills threshold required to obtain a work permit under the business and commercial scheme. An individual must now have:

a) a UK degree level qualification; or

b) A HND level occupational qualification which entitles the person to do a specific job; or

c) a general HND qualification plus one year's experience doing the type of job for which the permit is sought; or

d) at least 3 years high level specialist skills acquired doing the type of job for which the permit is sought. This type of job should be at NVQ level 3 or above.

From 1st November 2000, work permits can be awarded for up to 5 years. An indefinite leave to remain application can still be made after 4 years in the UK on a work permit.

At present the UK has on its SHORTAGE OCCUPATION LIST of the Overseas Labour Service at the Department for Education and Employment the following shortages:

- analyst programmers
- software engineers
- database specialists
- IT managers
- business analysts
- network specialists

- chartered engineers and physicists
- licensed aircraft engineers
- clinical psychologists
- pharmacists
- occupational therapists
- actuaries
- veterinary surgeons
- physiotherapists
- doctors (with defined specialisms)
- nurses (with defined specialisms)
- teachers (in London)

OTHER STATUTORY PROTECTION FOR EMPLOYEES

PROBLEM QUESTION:

Copehale Health Authority. advertised in the year 2003, internally, for a supervisor to take charge of domestic staff.

Annabel, who is 30 years old, worked for the Health Authority full time as a supervisor until 1998 when she left to have children.

She worked for the Health Authority from 1988 to 1998, ten years.

She now works part-time as a domestic auxiliary to fit in with the children.

She wants the job of supervisor but as a JOB SHARE.

She is not interviewed for the job because the Health Authority tells her that the post is not open to part-time staff, nor can the job be shared.

What problems does Copehale Health Authority face?

NOTICE, DISMISSAL AND REDUNDANCY

A contract of employment may be terminated in several ways:

1 by mutual agreement

2 by frustration

3 by expiry

4 b dismissal by the employer

5 by notice given by the employee or

6 by acceptance of a fundamental repudiatory breach of contract by the employer or the employee.

The distinction between these different kinds of termination will determine whether the employee can bring a claim for

- unfair dismissal

- wrongful dismissal or

- redundancy

The death of either party terminates the contract of employment, unless the contract expressly or impliedly provides otherwise.

The bankruptcy of the employer does not operate as a dissolution of the contracts of employment between himself and his employees, but in general, the winding up of a company and the dissolution of a partnership do operate to terminate the contract.

1 Termination by mutual agreement

Termination by agreement between employer and employee can be either orally or in writing. It can take place on any day in the month or year, not necessarily with a pay-day. But if the employee agrees to terminate his employment because of the threat of dismissal, he will be held to have been dismissed. If he had financial inducements to terminate his employment, it will be taken that he resigned by mutual consent but he will not be entitled to bring a claim for unfair dismissal or wrongful dismissal.

2 Termination by frustration

This occurs when the performance of the contract becomes impossible or if the performance is substantially different to what was agreed at the start of the contract. A contract will be terminated by frustration if performance becomes unlawful. Most often, frustration arises in cases of absence of the employee because of illness or imprisonment.

There is no dismissal in frustration. So there can be no claim for wrongful dismissal or unfair dismissal or redundancy.

3 Termination by expiry

If a contract is for a fixed period, it will automatically terminate at the end of that period. No notice need be given. But if an employee remains in employment after the expiry period, he will be considered to be working under the same terms and conditions as before and his employment is subject to an IMPLIED TERM THAT IT CAN BE TERMINATED by either party giving reasonable notice.

4 Dismissal by the employer

Dismissal is here used in its popular sense, to mean termination of a contract of employment by the employer. Dismissal may mean either SUMMARY or WITH NOTICE. Either party to the contract of employment is always free to terminate the relationship by giving the proper notice, provided that the contract is one which, whether expressly or impliedly, is terminable upon giving notice. If such notice is given, there can be no claim for WRONGFUL DISMISSAL. To be effective in law, the notice must expire on a certain specified day or on the occurrence of a specified event.

Unless the contract of employment provides for summary dismissal, summary dismissal is a breach of contract unless the employee is in fundamental breach of contract.

5 Termination by notice given by the employee

The statutory minimum period of notice to be given by an employee, who has been continuously employed for one month or more, is ONE WEEK (ERA 1996 section 86(2)). However the contractual period of notice to be given is usually longer. The contractual notice may be either expressly agreed upon or implied. If it is implied, the notice to be given is that which is a reasonable period in all circumstances.

If an employer is in breach of a fundamental term of the contract of employment, the employee is entitled to leave the employment forthwith. Leaving the employment in these circumstances is known as CONSTRUCTIVE DISMISSAL. In such circumstances the employee will be able to claim damages for WRONGFUL DISMISSAL.

6 Termination by repudiatory conduct

A breach of contract by either the employer or the employee entitles the other party to terminate the relationship without giving notice. It is of the nature of the employment relationship that, where one party is unwilling to perform the contract, it will be very difficult for the other party to say that the relationship remains alive. An acceptance of the breach will be inferred.

So, a repudiatory breach is a breach going to the root of the contract. Such a breach may have a variety of consequences. It may be a rejection of the original contract and bring into operation new terms, for example, a reduction in pay. In this situation, the innocent party has two options. First, he can treat the breach as terminating the contract and leave. Secondly, he can treat the breach as a variation in his terms and agree to continue the contract working under the new terms. In the second case there is a variation and as such no termination. In both the above cases it is the innocent party who makes the choice and the contract will not terminate until he accepts this as a consequence of the breach.

QUESTION 1

These events have taken place at St. David's Primary School.

Mr. Tonks, the PE teacher, was recently convicted of theft and sentenced to 2 years in prison.

During the time of the police investigation, Mr. Tonks was off sick for 3 months prior to his trial.

He appealed against the 2 year sentence one month later.

His sentence is reduced to 6 months.

At the time of his release his post as PE teacher had not been filled.

He is now claiming a redundancy payment.

St. David's school argued that Mr Tonks is no longer on the books.

Do you think that Mr. Tonks has been dismissed?

QUESTION 2

Emma worked at Erewhon University for ten years until she was dismissed five months ago for misconduct.

She was accused of stealing office supplies from the University.

A disciplinary hearing was held.

Emma did not ask her union representative to attend.

Emma appealed against the findings of the hearing.

There was no appeal hearing.

Can Emma claim unfair dismissal?

HEALTH AND SAFETY AT WORK

This is a rapidly developing section of the law. At common law, an employer is obliged to take such steps as are reasonably necessary to ensure the safety of his employees.
Where a job has inherent risks to health and safety which are not commonly known but of which the employer is aware or ought to be aware, he has a duty to inform prospective employees of this.

The employer must comply with his common law duty of care by:
-   providing a safe place of work

- providing a safe means of access to the place of work
- providing a safe system of work
- providing adequate equipment and materials
- employing competent fellow employees, and,
- protecting employees from unnecessary risk of injury.

Occupier's Liability Act 1957

Apart from the common law duties of an employer to provide his employees with a safe place of work, as an occupier of premises, he owes his employees, and other visitors, the common law duty of care imposed by the Occupiers Liability Act 1957. The extent of the duty owed to trespassers is defined by the Occupiers Liability Act 1984.

Health and Safety at Work Act 1975

An employer is obliged to take such steps as are reasonably necessary to ensure the safety of his employees. Where a job has inherent risks to health and safety which are not commonly known but of which the employer is or ought to be aware, and if the employer cannot guard against these risks by taking precautionary measures, then he has a duty to inform prospective employees of the risks. The employer must keep abreast of contemporary knowledge in the field of accident prevention.

The employer has to comply with the following:

a) providing a safe place of work
b) providing a safe means of access to the place of work
c) providing a safe system of work
d) providing adequate equipment and materials
e) employing competent fellow employees and
f) protecting employees from unnecessary risk of injury.

The HSWA 1974 section 33 specifies offences and in 2003 the Government set out new maximum penalties for these section 33 offences.

HSWA section	new MAX penalty
section 33(1)(a)	SUMMARY
general duties on employers & others	6 months prison or £20,000 max fine
Section 33(1)(a)	
duty on employees	6 months prison or £5,000 max fine
Section 33(1)(b)	
duty not to interfere with or misuse health & safety things	6 months prison or £20,000 max fine

The Health and Safety at Work Act 1974 lays down general principles to be followed by employers. It governs the health and safety at work of employees. It establishes the Health and Safety Commission and the Health and Safety Executive. It gives powers to inspectors to issue improvement notices and prohibition notices and imposes some civil and criminal liabilities upon employers.

THE HEALTH AND SAFETY AT WORK ACT

New Maximum Penalties for Health and Safety at Work Offences(2003)

HSWA Section	Maximum Penalty
33(1)(a) the duties on employers and others	6 months prison or fine up to £20,000
33(1)(a) duty on employees	6 months prison or fine up to £5,000.
33(1)(b) duty not to interfere with or misuse things provided for health and safety	6 months prison or fine up to £20,000.
33(1)(b) duty not to charge employees for things done to meet statutory requirements	fine up to £20,000

33(1)(c)
contravening requirements of health and safety regulations

6 months prison or fine up to £20,000

33(1)(d)
contravening requirements imposed in relation to special investigations, etc

fine up to £5,000

33(1)(e)
contravening any requirement under section 20

6 months prison or fine up to £20,000

33(1)(f)
preventing another person from appearing before an inspector

6 months prison or fine up to £20,000

33(1)(g)
contravening an improvement or prohibition notice

6 months prison or fine up to £20,000

33(1)(h)
obstructing an inspector

6 months prison or fine up to £5,000

33(1)(I)
contravening any notice issued under section 27(1)

fine up to £5,000

33(1)(j)
disclosing information in breach of section 27(4)

6 months prison or fine up to £5,000 or both

33(1)(k),(l),(m)
offences relating to deception

6 months prison or fine up to £20,000

33(1)(n)
falsely to pretend to be an inspector

fine up to £5,000

33(1)(o)
failure to comply with a court remedy

6 months prison or fine up to £20,000

33(3)
penalties for health and safety offences arising from existing statutory provisions (pre 1974 HSWA)

6 months prison or fine up to £20,000

33(4)(a),(b),(c)
offence of breaching licensing or explosives requirement

6 months prison or fine up to £20,000

Personal liability of directors and other company officers

Under HSWA 1974, section 37, personal liability is imposed on any director, manager or other similar officer of a company if an offence is committed by the company under HSWA 1974, or any other health and safety legislation specified in HSWA 1974, Schedule 1, due to the neglect or with the consent or connivance, of any such person.

See cases   Tesco Supermarkets Ltd v Nattrass [1972] AC 153
                 R v Boal [1992] IRLR 420

A director found guilty of an indictable offence under the HSWA 1974, may be disqualified from holding office as a director under the Company Disqualification Act 1986, section 2(1).

Corporate Killing

Under the current law a conviction for corporate manslaughter is obtainable only where a senior individual in a company is shown to have been grossly negligent and so responsible for the fatal accident.

The first conviction for corporate manslaughter was in 1994 where the managing director who personally controlled an activity centre was held responsible for the deaths of four children in his company's care while on a canoeing trip.

In 1996 there was another conviction for corporate manslaughter, resulting in the imprisonment of the managing director of a transport company after an employee was killed while cleaning chemical residues from a road tanker without protective equipment.

QUESTION

Employment Law—Health and Safety ; Dismissal Issues.

Coppenhall Ltd is a company manufacturing sheet metal. Last year, the company manufacturing sheet metal. Last year, the company placed the workforce on a 4 day week in an attempt to reduce costs while maintaining productivity. Work in the factory is hard and involves a lot of heavy lifting of sheets of metal weighing between 40 KGs and 60 Kgs each. Workers are advised to life such sheets in pairs but are unsupervised in their work. Management provides waist belts to reduce the risk of injury. The belts are available on request, but, as the company knows, they are rarely worn in practice.

Michael has worked for Coppenhall for 18 months and has complained to management that the change to a 4 day week has created additional safety risks on the shop floor. Management has not followed up these complaints. Michael, in fact, strained his back when he first started work, in a lifting accident, an event of which management are aware, but Michael never wears a waist belt.

Two months ago, as no assistance was readily available, Michael attempted to life a 60Kgs sheet of metal unaided, and in doing so, slipped a disc in his back. Due to his previous injury, this recent accident will lead to him having permanent future back problems. Michael has now resigned from his job and wishes to sue Coppenhall for compensation.

What do you think Michael's position is??

Criminalisation of employers' conduct

Statute has intervened to criminalize the conduct of those who use their position as directors to benefit themselves through the insider dealing legislation, for example. Sections 52 and 57(2) of the Criminal Justice Act 1993 refers to and prohibits directors from dealing in shares on the basis of inside information they gained from their positions.

Directors must show the duty of skill and care. (<u>Lagunas Nitrate Co v Lagunas Syndicate [1989]</u>).

In the absence of any grounds of suspicion, directors are entitled to leave the day to day operation of the company's business in the hands of managers and to trust them to perform their tasks honestly.

HOW DOES THE HUMAN RIGHTS ACT AFFECT EMPLOYMENT LAW?

The HRA is targeted at the misuse of power by the State.
It does not directly protect employees against the acts of private employers.
Public Authorities must act in conformity with the Convention.
Government departments
local authorities
Articles 4 (prohibition of slavery and forced labour), article 11(freedom of association), and articles 6,8,9,10 and 14 apply.

BUSINESS STRUCTURES

PARTNERSHIPS

Partners enter into an agreement on terms that they themselves have negotiated. They are contractually bound by those terms., which must not conflict with the express terms of the Partnership Act 1890. The partnership usually has an Articles of Partnership.

The Articles of Partnership will cover such matters as

- the nature of the business
- the name of the firm
- capital contributions to be made by individual partners
- business accounts
- how to share profits
- dissolution of the partnership.

General principles

Much of the law relating to partnership is to be found in the Partnership Act 1890. (I have put a copy of this on WOLF. It will stay there until May 2004 to help you to write your assignment 2).

The Partnership Act stated the law as it had developed up to 1890 but cases decided before 1890 may still be used as an aid to help you understand the Act.

The Partnership Act does NOT provide a complete code of partnership law. Section 46 specifically states that:

"The rules of equity and of common law applicable to partnership shall continue in force except so far as they are consistent with the express provisions of this Act".

This is why we now have The Partnership Act 2000 which deals specifically with a new concept, limited liability partnerships.

What is a partnership?

The definition of a partnership is found in section 1(1) PA 1890:

"Partnership is the relation which subsists between persons carrying on a business in common with a view to profit."

So, for example, a registered limited company is NOT a partnership. A partnership is when two or more persons carry on a business. Section 45 PA 1890 defines "business".

According to section 45 PA 1890, a business includes "every trade, occupation or profession"

Section 2 PA 1890 lays down certain rules that determine whether a business is a partnership. Section 2 states that:

a) Joint or common ownership of property does not of itself create a partnership, even where profits from the property are shared. (s 2(1)).

b) The sharing of GROSS returns does not of itself create a partnership. (section 2(2)). A person is not, therefore, a partner in a business merely because he receives commission on sales which he introduced.

c) The receipt of a share of profits is prima facie evidence of partnership Section 2(3)).

The presence or absence of a written partnership agreement is NOT conclusive evidence as to whether or not there is a partnership. The existence of a partnership is always a question of fact.

So, a partnership is, in law, very different from a limited company. In commercial terms the most significant difference is that partners have unlimited liability for the debts of the partnership, unless the partnership was a new limited liability partnership (LLP).

Partnerships are not required to be registered in any way that companies are. They are NOT required to make public their accounts like limited companies are.

A partnership is not a separate legal entity like a limited company is. The partnership consists of the individuals who together form the partnership.

The maximum number of persons who can be in a partnership is 20.

This is because section 716 CA 1985 prohibits the formation of business associations with more than 20 members unless they are registered as companies under the CA 1985.

Section 716(2) CA 1985 gives exceptions to this rule to accountants and solicitors.

Capacity

Any person is legally capable of forming a partnership with any other person. Companies as well as individuals can, provided their objects clause gives them the power to do so, enter a partnership with other companies or with individuals.

Minors (persons under 18) are capable of entering into a partnership. But if the minor wishes to void the contract he can do so up to age 18 and he is not liable for the debts of the partnership if these were incurred during his minority but he can claim his share of any partnership property in priority to the firm's creditors.

Duration of partnership

Most partnerships are partnerships at will. This means that no particular period is agreed upon as being the time during which the partnership is to last.

A partnership at will can be dissolved by notice unless there is an agreement to the contrary. It is also possible to have a partnership for a fixed term or a partnership for a term defined by reference to some event, for example, the completion of some particular job but this kind of partnership cannot be dissolved by notice. The beginning of a partnership is a question of fact.

Partnership name and publicity of information

A partnership is entitled to choose any name which it wishes. The law relating to partnership names is contained in the Business Names Act 1985. The Act permits the free use of certain names and requires approval of others.

Automatically permitted names

If the business of a partnership is carried on under a name which consists of the surnames of all the partners no restrictions apply. (section 1 Business Names Act 1985). This is true also if the names consists of surnames together with permitted additions and nothing else. The permitted additions are the forenames or the initials of the partners, the addition of an S to a surname to signify that there is more than one partner with that same name and/or a statement that the business is being carried on in succession to the business of a former owner. In other cases, approval of the name is required under section 2 and section 3 of The Business Names Act 1985.

Section 2 of the Business Names Act 1985 makes it an offence to carry on a business (without approval of the Secretary of State) under a name which suggests a connection with the government or a local authority or which includes a word specified in regulations made under the Act.

Regulations have been made under the Act which specif scores of words for which approval is required. Words such as BUILDING SOCIETY, SHEFFIELD, WORDS CONNOTING CONNECTION WITH THE VARIOUS MEDICAL PROFESSIONS.

Partners who are starting a business or who wish to use a business name should consult the regulations. If they find that their name includes a word covered by the regulations they should first write to the government department or other body which is to be consulted in relation to that word asking it whether it objects. They should then apply to the Secretary of State for approval stating that they have made such a request and enclosing a copy of any reply that they have received from the government department or other body that they have consulted.

Any partnership which uses a business name other than one permitted under section 1 Business Names Act 1985, is required to state the name of each partner (together with an address for service in Great Britain) on every business letter, order for goods or services, invoice, receipt and written demand for payment of a debt Section 4(1)(a) Business Names Act 1985).

The same information must also be given *by a notice* in a prominent position at each place of business of the partnership (section 4(1)(b) Business Names Act 1985)

The same information must be given *in writing* to anyone with whom the partnership has had dealings or negotiations and who asks for the information (section 4(2) Business Names Act 1985). This disclosure requirement does not apply to a partnership to more than 20 members provided that NONE of the partners' names appear (other than as signatories) and provided the letter includes a statement of the address of the principal place of business and a statement that the name and addresses of the partners can be inspected there.

The partnership deed or agreement

Partners enter into the agreement on the terms that they themselves have negotiated. So they are contractually bound by those terms, as long as those terms do not expressly conflict with the provisions in the Partnership Act 1890. These terms may be enforced by the law in the same way as other contractual terms.

Usually the terms are set out in the form of Articles of Partnership and any gaps in the Articles will be filled by reference to the Partnership Act 1890.

These terms will be terms about
-   The nature of the business to be transacted
-   The name of the firm
-   The capital contributions to be made by individual partners
-   The drawing up of the business accounts
-   The method of determining and sharing profits
-   The law imposes duties on partners ; these are the fiduciary duties of partners.

A written agreement is NOT required for the formation of a partnership. This contrasts with the position of a company where the memorandum and articles, which have contractual effect under section 14 Companies Act 1985, must not only be in writing but must also be registered with the Registrar of Companies.

In practice many partnerships decide that the agreement between the partners, as to how the business is regulated, should be in the form of a written agreement. Such an agreement is often called a **partnership agreement**, a **partnership deed** or **articles of partnership**.

When writing a partnership deed, you must bear in mind that many of the provisions in the Partnership Act 1890 are there to regulate the relationship of the partners EXCEPT to the extent that there is a contrary agreement. The nature of a partnership agreement must depend upon the circumstances.

Points to note when drafting a partnership deed:

1.   THE PARTIES
The deed will specify who are the partners and may make provision for the admission of new partners. If the deed does not make such provisions, then-new partners may only be admitted with the unanimous consent of the existing partners (section 24(7) Partnership Act 1890).

2.   THE NATURE OF BUSINESS.
There is no rule that says you must specify this. But it is a good idea to specify this in the deed so that if one partner objects to what is being done by way of new types of business, he can insist on the deed being followed. If there is a clause that specifies exactly what the business does, it can only be altered with the unanimous agreement of all the partners. (s24(8) PA 1890). This clause can also include WHERE the partnership is to carry on business.

3.   NAME
The business name of the partnership should be specified.

4.   CAPITAL.
A clause, or group of clauses, should be included dealing with the financial relationships between the partners. This should state what investment each partner is to make in the business, what, if any, return he is to get on his investment in the form of interest on capital, whether he is to be entitled to a salary and, how any profits or losses are to be ascertained or divided. Also what is to happen to the partnership assets on dissolution.

5. PROPERTY

Provision should be made specifying which property is to be regarded as partnership property and which is to remain the property of individual partners.

6. MANAGEMENT

Small partnerships of 2 or 3 people will usually be run by the partners. There may also be some employees. Each partner will have an equal say in management.

In a large partnership, such a large firms of solicitors or accountants, a more complex management structure should be specified. Unless the partnership deed states otherwise, all partners have an equal say in management.

The clauses must contain such items as who is entitled to sign the cheques,

Who will allocate the work to employees,

What authority each partner is to have with regards to buying stock, paying bills, etc. In big partnerships the deed could state that, for example, all junior partners are to have such functions as are assigned to them by the managing or senior partners, rather than list minute details in the deed.

7. DISSOLUTION.

The deed should include terms dealing with the dissolution of the partnership and clauses to provide for what is to happen in case of death or retirement of partners.

8. RESTRICTIONS

The deed may have terms which deal with the partners' obligations to the firm (eg confidentiality, loyalty, etc).

Also, terms such as that the partners are to give their whole time to the business of the firm or a clause to state that partners must only take up other businesses with the approval of their partners, a clause to prevent each partner from doing business in competition with the firm during the continuance of the partnership, even if the partners are not full time. Another good clause to have in the deed is a restrictive covenant preventing competition with the firm by a partner after he has left the firm, as long as this clause does not make unreasonable demands.

Duties of partners

SOME of the duties of partners are set out in the Partnership Act 1890:

Section 10—the liability of partners in regard to torts, is JOINT AND SEVERAL. But the wrong sued on must have been committed in the ordinary course of the partnership business.

Section 25—no majority of partners can expel another partner, unless such power is contained in the partnership agreement.

Section 28 states that partners must provide true accounts and give full information to the other partners in relation to all things affecting the partnership. This may be cited as a general DUTY OF DISCLOSURE, and its application may be seen in Law v Law [1905] All ER 526, CA, in which the court held that an agreement to transfer a share in a partnership could have been set aside because the partner buying did not disclose the value of particular assets to the partner selling.

Section 29 provides that partners must account to the firm for any benefit obtained, without consent, from any transaction relating to the partnership. It is necessary to make full disclosure so that individual profits can be seen. This DUTY TO ACCOUNT may be seen in Bentley v Craven [1853] 52 ER 29, in which a partner bought goods on his own account and later sold them to the partnership at a profit, without declaring his interest to the other partners. As a result, the partnership was entitled to recover the profit from the defendant.

Section 30 states that a partner must not compete with the partnership business, without the consent of the other partners.
Any breach of this duty NOT TO COMPETE will render the competing partner liable to account to the partnership for any profits made in the course of competition.

Partners cannot enter into contracts with their partnership enterprise.

Limited liability partnerships

Since 6th April 2001 any two persons (individuals or companies) may form a limited liability partnership. LLP. The LLP is sometimes called a private company.

This is an entirely new concept which came into being as the result initially, of pressure from the larger accountancy firms concerned by the potential liability of partners for substantial damages awarded against them for the negligence of one partner, often in a totally different office.

LLP's are formed under the Limited Liability Partnership Act 2000 which came into effect on 6th April 2001.
All of the Insolvency Act as it applies to the winding up of companies and the Company Directors Disqualification Act applies to LLP's. The majority of the law applicable to LLP's is company law and not Partnership law. So an LLP is a modified form of a private company. It is not a partnership with limited liability.

Section 1(5) of the LLP Act says that partnership law shall not apply to LLP's UNLESS express provision is made to the contrary.
An LLP does NOT have shareholders, directors or share capital. It is up to the members to regulate their internal affairs by agreement.
The regulations also apply certain provisions of the Financial Services and Markets Act 2000 to LLP's.

Section 1 of the LLP Act creates the LLP as a body corporate. Therefore an LLP has legal personality distinct from that of its members. The LLP alone will be liable for its debts. It will be the contracting party.
It may be liable for the acts of its agents.

The LLP is therefore a body corporate and is liable for its own debts. So its members, like shareholders in the case of a limited company, only have exposure to liability for those debts up to their financial interests in the LLP.
This will include vicarious liability, eg, the negligence of one of its members.

The Sex Discrimination Act, the Race Relations Act, the Business Names Act all apply to LLP's for litigation purposes.

BUT for tax purposes section 10 of the LLP Act states that where an LLP is carrying on a trade, profession or business with a view to profit it will be taxed for income tax and capital gains tax purposes as if it were a partnership and not a company. So tax liability will be on the members for their income and gains derived from the LLP.

Where LLP's are formed for non-business purposes they will taxed as companies under the Companies Act.

FORMATION OF AN LLP

To form an LLP you must complete an application form to become incorporated. The process is governed by sections 2 and 3 of the LLP Act. To incorporate an LLP you must deliver certain documents to the registrar of companies, who ill register it and issue a certificate of incorporation.

Section 2(1) tells you the requirements for incorporation. Fill in an incorporation document.

Deliver it to the registrar of companies.

Two or more persons must sign that they are "associated for carrying on a lawful business with a view to profit".

Then a solicitor must sign that they are formed to carrying on business with a view to profit.

Registration of this document puts it in the public domain.

This document must contain 5 items of information (LLP Act section 2(2)).

1. The name of the LLP. It must have the suffix LLP at the end of its name.

2. It must state the registered office of the LLP. It must give the actual address.

3. You cannot change this address unless you report this to the Companies House Registrar.

4. The document must set out the names and addresses of the initial members of the LLP.

5. It must state which members are to be regarded as "designated members".

Any new members must give their names, addresses and DOB to the registrar within 28 days. (s 288 Companies act 1985).

Once registered the LLP will be given a number, the registered information will be open to public inspection, fees will be payable, electronic communications possible and the fact of the incorporation will be published by the registrar in the London and Edinburgh Gazette.

Designated members are those under section 8 of the LLP Act who are specified as such in the incorporation document or who subsequently became designated members in accordance with the LLP agreement. There must be at

least 2 designated members, and in default, all the members become designated members. Designated members have responsibility for
the signing of accounts,
filing the accounts with the registrar,
the appointment and removal of auditors,
applications for the striking off of the LLP from the register and
they are liable for failing to deliver the annual return.

FINANCIAL AND OTHER CONTROLS
LLP regulations have applied 5 areas of company law regulation to LLP's.

1. Duty to prepare and file audited accounts;

2. The requirements as to the appointment of auditors;

3. The duty to prepare and file an annual return;

4. The need to identify the LLP on correspondence,etc';

5. Thepossibility of a DTI investigation into the affairs, etc.of an LLP.

With regarde to the filing of audited accounts with the registrar, the whole of Part VII of the Companies Act applies to LLP's.
LIABILITY FOR CONTRACTS, TORTS AND OTHER WRONGS

Like a company, an LLP as a body corporate will be able to make its own contracts. But it can only do so in one of two ways:
Unser s 36 Companies Act, by wringing, under its common seal; and by any person acting under its implied or express authority.

With regard to torts, crimes and breach of trust, (s6(4) LLP ACT) the LLP is vicariously liable for any wrongful act or omission committed by a member in the course of the business of the LLP or with its authority.

DUTIES OF MEMBERS TO THE LLP
Section 5(1) of the LLP Act provides that,
The mutual rights and duties of the members of an LLP shall be governed by

a) agreement between the members, or between the LLP and its members;

b) or in the absence of agreement as to any matter, by any provision made in relation to that matter, by regulations under section 15 (c).

CESSATION OF MEMBERSHIP

This may be amicable or it may result from some sort of breakdown of relationships between the members.

Cessation can be by agreement or by notice. Section 4(3) LLP ACT states that any member may cease to be such in accordance with an agreement with the other members. So membership is at the will of the member. If someone ceases to be a member, the others do not have to buy out his share as in a partnership. So, unless there is a minority protection provision, a ceased member may be in limbo. As soon as the registrar is notified that someone has ceased to be a member of the LLP, they are deemed to no longer be a member of the LLP.

A member will cease automatically if

He dies;

He becomes bankrupt;

He grants a trust deed for the benefit of creditors or

He assigns the whole or part of his share in the LLP.

As an ex-member, he cannot interfere in the management or admin of the LLP. If he is bankrupt, the trustee in bankruptcy cannot interfere either.

A member can also cease by being expelled from the LLP if the agreement has express powers to do so.

WINDING UP AND INSOLVENCY

Regulation 5 of the LLP Regulations applies virtually all the provisions of the Insolvency Act.

LLP can make voluntary arrangements, be subject to administration orders, be in receivership and be wound up in the same way as companies.

Specimen partnership deed

ACKNOWLEDGMENT AND DISCLAIMER

This specimen is taken from Kelly's Draftsman 18th Editions published by Butterworths. It is produced as an example of the kind of clauses often used in partnership deeds but it is not applicable or to be used in any particular case. The author does not accept any responsibility for anything that any person does or does not do as a result of reading it.

THIS DEED is made on (*date*)
between:

I.   (*name*) of (*address*) ("xxxxx");

II. (*name*) of (*address*) ("xxxxx");

III. (*name*) of (*address*) ("xxxxx");

IV. (*name*) of (*address*) ("xxxxx"); and

V. (*name*) of (*address*) ("xxxxx").

Part 1: Introduction

(1) DEFINITIONS

(i) In this deed the following terms shall have the following meanings.

'1890 Act'	means the Partnership Act 1890.
'Accounting Year'	means the Partnership accounting year which ends on (*date*).
'Business'	means the business of (*description*) [intended to be] carried on by the Partners.
'Continuing Partners'	means the Partners except a Former Partner.
'Effective Date'	means (*date*).
'Former Partner'	means a person who whilst a Partner retires, is expelled [becomes bankrupt] or dies.
'Lease'	means a lease [of the Property] dated (*date*) and made between (*name*) and (*name*).
'Partners'	means (*name*), (*name*) and (*name*).
'Partnership'	means the Partnership created by this deed.
'Property'	means the property known as (*address*) with registered title number (*number*) (*or*) comprised in the deed dated (*date*).
'Seller'	means a person in respect of whom a Relevant Event occurs or his personal representatives or receiver.
'a Relevant Event'	occurs when and if a Partner retires, is expelled from the Partnership[, becomes bankrupt or a patient under the Mental Health Act 1983] or dies.

'becomes bankrupt'	in respect of any person means is declared bankrupt by a court or has an administration order made against [him] and other forms of the word and cognate expressions shall have corresponding meanings.
'clause' and 'schedule'	mean respectively clauses or schedules in this deed unless the context shows a contrary meaning.
'now' and 'today'	mean at the date of this deed.
'observe'	includes 'perform'.
'parties'	means the parties to this deed.

Part 2: Establishment

(1) FORMATION OF PARTNERSHIP

(i) The Partners agree to become partners in the Business on the terms of this deed.

(2) COMMENCEMENT

(i) This deed takes effect on and from [the Commencement Date (*or*) (*date*) (*or*) today].

(3) NAME

(i) The name of the Partnership shall be '(*name*)'.

Part 3: Financial

(4) CAPITAL

(i) The capital of the Partnership shall be £(.....) ((.....) pounds) (100%) which shall be contributed by and belong to the Partners as [appears opposite their names in the schedule (*or*) as follows]:

as to £(.....) ((.....) pounds) ((*amount*)%) to (*name*),

as to £(.....) ((.....) pounds) ((*amount*)%) to (*name*), and

as to £(.....) ((.....) pounds) ((*amount*)%) to (*name*).

(5) LEASEHOLD PROPERTY

(i) The leasehold office premises known as (*address-A*) and (*address-B*) and any other premises leased or acquired in connection with the Partnership shall be held by those Partners in whose names the legal estates are vested in trust for the Partners as tenants in common in the shares in which they are entitled to the Partnership capital. The Partnership shall pay and discharge all liabilities and outgoings and perform and observe all covenants and other obligations in respect of these premises and compensate in full on demand the Partners, in whom the legal estates are vested, for all claims and liabilities in respect of the premises, except their respective liabilities as Partners.

(6) INTEREST ON CAPITAL

(i) Each Partner shall be credited with interest on his share in the capital the first day of each Accounting Year at the Rate of Interest on the last day of each Accounting Year before any division of profits is made.

(7) PROFITS AND LOSSES

(i) The Partnership's profits and losses (including profits and losses of capital) shall be divided between and borne by the Partners in proportion to the shares in its capital for the time being owned by them.

(8) DIRECTORSHIPS AND OTHER INCOME

(i) All remuneration or other emoluments from any source (except as mentioned below) received by a Partner shall be treated as the income of the Partnership. Remuneration or other emoluments in this clause includes, but is not limited to, profits from any business, fees or other reward for work done or in respect of directorships and other offices of a public or private nature, lecture fees and royalties for papers and books published, but shall not include:

(b) interest and dividends paid on bank and similar accounts or in respect of investments of a passive nature in which the Partner has no management or other role;

(c) director's fees received by (*name-A*) in respect of [his] directorship of (*name*) Ltd; and

(d) income received by any Partner, which has been agreed in advance by [the other Partners (*or*) the Senior Partner].

(9) DRAWINGS ON ACCOUNT OF PROFITS

    (a) Each Partner may draw not more than £(.....) ((.....) pounds) a month on account of [his] share of profits.

    (b) If on the taking of the general annual account the drawings of any Partner during any Accounting Year are found to exceed his share in the profits for that year [with interest on his capital] he shall refund the excess immediately with interest at the Rate of Interest on the excess from the end of the Accounting Year until payment.

(10) DIVISION OF PROFITS

(i) As soon as the annual accounts have been signed by the Partners the net profits (if any) of the business shall be divisible between them in the proportions in which they owned the capital of the Partnership or are entitled to share in the profits and losses of the Partnership after:

    (b) transferring to a separate reserve or bank account or other investment agreed by the Partners an amount calculated by the Partnership's accountants to be with any other amounts previously transferred sufficient to discharge the whole amount of income tax payable in respect of the Partnership's profits for all years of assessment ending before the last day of the accounting year in respect of which the accounts were prepared; and

    (c) paying in respect of each Partner [a contribution of not less than [17.5]% of his not relevant earnings from the Partnership to (or) the maximum contribution which that Partner may, by reference to his net relevant earnings from the Partnership in the year just ended, pay under one or more personal pension policies or retirement annuity contracts (approved respectively under Chapters IV and III of Part XIV of the Income and Corporation Taxes Act 1988)].

(11) HOLIDAYS

(i) Each Partner shall be entitled to [4] weeks' holiday in each year at the time or times agreed between them of which not more than [3] weeks shall be taken consecutively and between April to October inclusive and of which at least one week shall be taken between November to March inclusive.

(12) CARS

(i) The following cars shall be available for use by the Partners and all expenses of insuring, taxing, maintaining, repairing and running them shall be paid by the Partnership as Partnership expenses:

> (*name*) make and model.
>
> (*name*) make and model; and
>
> (*name*) make and model.

(13) MATERNITY

(a) A Partner who becomes pregnant shall be entitled to up to [six] months leave of absence. Up to eleven weeks may be taken prior to the expected date of confinement but the period of leave may commence earlier if a doctor certifies that it should. This absence shall not affect the Partner's holiday entitlement.

(b) A Partner who becomes pregnant shall give to her other partners as much notice as is reasonable in the circumstances of:

> (a) her expected date of confinement;
>
> (b) the date on which she expects to leave work; and
>
> (c) the date on which she expects to return to work.

(c) If a Partner becomes pregnant:

> (a) for the first three months of absence she shall be entitled to her full share of profits;
>
> (b) for the next three months she shall be entitled to one half of her full share of profits; and
>
> (c) for any further period of absence she shall not be entitled to any further share of profits, unless [the absence arises through sickness (in which case the provisions of this deed for sick leave shall apply) or] otherwise agreed from time to time.

Part 4: Conduct of partnership

(14) PLACE OF BUSINESS

(i) The business of the Partnership shall be carried on at the Property (*or*) (*address-Λ*) or at such other place or places as the Partners from time to time agree.

(15) SENIOR PARTNER

(i)   The senior partner of the Partnership shall be (*name*) and he shall be responsible for and have the power of final decision in all matters of day to day management[, but [his] powers under this clause shall not extend to the matters mentioned in clause [18]].

(16) PARTNERSHIP MEETINGS

(i)   The Partners shall meet not less than once in every [two months] at times to be determined reasonably by the Senior Partner, but any Partner or Partners [whose profit shares (or, if more than one, aggregate profit shares) are not less than [10]%] may convene a Partnership meeting at any time on at least two days' written notice.

(17) PARTNERSHIP DECISIONS

(a)   Unless otherwise agreed unanimously by the Partners, decisions on the following matters shall be taken only by a meeting of the Partners:

(a)   the admission of new Partners;

(b)   the expulsion of a Partner;

(c)   any increase in the Partnership's capital;

(d)   any alteration to the shares of the Partners in the Partnership's profits and losses;

(e)   any borrowing by the Partnership except within the limits of any overdraft facility agreed by the Partners and the Partnership's bank;

(f)   any acquisition or disposal of premises for the Partnership or the opening or closing of branch offices;

(g)   any change in the Partnership's bank or the terms of its arrangements for operating its bank accounts;

(h)   any change in the Partnership's auditors;

(i)   the engagement or dismissal of any legally qualified staff;

(j)   the acquisition or disposal of any asset of a value in excess of £(...)((...) *pounds*);

(k)   any compromise or other settlement of any claim against the partnership or its insurers by a third party.

(b) Decisions of the Partners at Partnership meetings may be made by a majority of at least [[four fifths] of the Partners (*or*) Partners holding between them a share of [80]% of the Partnership profits]. A Partner who is unable to attend a Partnership meeting may appoint another Partner as his representative with power to speak and vote for him and shall be bound by any vote made on his behalf by his representative.

(18) BANK

(i) The Partnership bank shall be (*name*) Bank plc (*address*) branch and all cheques shall be signed by at least [two] Partners.

(19) ACCOUNTS

(i) The Partners shall keep all necessary and proper account of the Partnership's transactions and on (*date*) in every year an account shall be taken of the Partnership's assets and liabilities and its profits and losses [(including profits and losses earned or incurred but not actually received or paid) (*or*) (but so that actual receipts and payments alone shall be taken into account)] for the preceding year and shall be signed by each Partner.

(ii) Accounts when signed shall be conclusive and final between the Partners as to all matters stated in them unless some manifest error is discovered within three months after they have been signed, in which case the error shall be rectified.

(20) GOOD FAITH

(a) Each Partner shall:

(a) the devote [his] whole time and attention to the Partnership business (except during holidays and absences because of illness or injury);

(b) employ himself diligently in the Partnership;

(c) use [his] best endeavours to promote its interests;

(d) punctually pay and discharge [his] separate debts and engagements and compensate the other Partner and the Partnership assets in full on demand for all liabilities in respect of them; and

(e) be just and faithful to the other Partner in all transactions relating to the Partnership and at all times give to the other a true account of all such dealings.

(b) No Partner shall without the consent of the other[s]:

(a) engage or be concerned or interested either directly or indirectly in any other business or occupation;

(b) engage or make any contract with or dismiss any employee;

(c) enter into any engagement as a result of which the Partners may risk the loss of or be made liable for one sum or any number of sums in respect of the same transaction amounting to £(…..) ((…..) pounds) or more;

(d) forgive the whole or any part of any debt or sum due to the Partners;

(e) except in the ordinary course of trade dispose by loan, pledge, sale or otherwise of any part of the Partnership property;

(f) become bail guarantor or surety for any person or do or knowingly suffer anything as a result of which the Partnership property may be endangered;

(g) assign or charge his interest in the Partnership; or

(h) draw or accept or endorse any bill of exchange or promissory note on account of the Partnership.

Part 5: Termination

(21) TERMINATION

(a) The Partnership may be terminated by [either (*or*) any] Partner giving to the other[s] [not less than (*number*) months' written notice expiring on any anniversary of the commencement of the Partnership (*or*) not earlier than (number) years from the Effective Date] and at the end of that notice the Partnership shall terminate.

(b) Any Partner may retire at any time on not less than [six] months' written notice to the other Partners and on his retirement he shall cease to be a Partner but the Partnership shall continue between the other Partners.

(22) EXPULSION

(i)   If:

    (b) any money payable by a Partner to the other Partners under this deed is in arrears for (*number*) days [whether legally demanded or not];

    (c) any Partner fails to comply in all material respects with this deed;

    (d) any Partner fails to comply with any of [his] obligations under this deed or any deed supplemental to it [and the failure (if capable of being remedied) remains unremedied for [10] days after being called to [his] attention by written notice from the party not in default];

    (e) any circumstances arise which give reasonable grounds in the other Partner's opinion for [his] belief that a Partner has or may become incapable of performing [his] obligations under this deed;

    (f) any Partner is unable or prevented from carrying out [his] duties under this deed through incapacity or any other cause for any period or periods exceeding a total of (*number*) [weeks] in any period of (*number*) [weeks];

    (g) any Partner becomes of unsound mind or a patient within the meaning of the Mental Health Act 1983;

    (h) any Partner is convicted of any criminal offence other than an offence which in the reasonable opinion of the other Partner's does not affect [his] relation to the other Partners under this deed;

    (i) any Partner ceases to hold any licence or professional qualification or has [his] name removed from any register which is or which the other Partner's consider necessary or desirable for the performance of [his] duties under this deed;

    (j) any Partner becomes bankrupt, has a receiving order made against [him], makes any arrangement with [his] creditors generally or takes or suffers any similar action as a result of debt;

    (k) a receiver or administrative receiver is appointed of any Partner's property;

    (l) any execution is levied upon any Partners goods or on the Property;

    (m) any Partner purports to assign the burden or benefits or charge the benefits of this deed; or

    (n) any Partner is guilty of any grave misconduct or wilful neglect in the discharge of the Partnership's duties under this agreement;

(ii) the other Partners may by a written notice signed by [all (*or*) not less than [80]% (*or*) all except one] of them expel him from the Partnership on the date specified in the notice.

Part 6: Devolution and payment

(23) DISSOLUTION

(i) If the option under the following clauses to purchase the Former Partner's share is not exercised by the Continuing Partners, the Partnership shall be wound up and its assets sold as provided by the 1890 Act but so that each Partner shall be at liberty to bid at any sale of any Partnership assets.

(24) OPTION TO BUY

(i) On a Relevant Event the Continuing Partners shall have the option (to be exercised by written notice to the Seller not later than [one month] after the Relevant Event) to buy the Former Partner's share in the Partnership's capital as at the date of the Relevant Event.

(25) FURTHER ASSURANCE

(i) The Seller shall execute all documents and do all things which the (*Party-B*) requires to vest in the (*Party-B*) the full rights, title and interest in the (*subject matter*) [or to confer on the (*Party-B*) all rights of action whether accruing before or after the date of this deed in relation to any infringement of the (*subject matter*) or any rights in it].

(26) PRICE AND PAYMENT

(a) The price of the Former Partner's share in the Partnership shall be certified in writing by the Partnership's auditors as soon as possible after the Relevant Event and the certificate shall be binding on and conclusive against the Continuing Partners and the Seller. In assessing the price the auditors shall take account of:

   (a) the value of the Partnership's assets and liabilities [including (*or*) excluding] goodwill and profits and losses earned or incurred but not actually received or paid,

   (b) drawings by the Former Partner since the end of the last Accounting Year and any money owing by [him] to the Partnership, and

(c) the fact that all the Partnership's liabilities at the Relevant Event are to be discharged by the Continuing Partners.

(b) The Continuing Partners shall pay the price as follows:

(a) [the amount payable in place of current profits on the exercise of the option,]

(b) the balance by [twelve] equal instalments at intervals of [three] months in arrears from the date of the Relevant Event (*or*) exercise of the option; and

(c) interest on the amount from time to time unpaid at the Rate of Interest from the date of the Relevant Event until payment payable in arrears on each date on which instalments are payable.

(c) The balance of the price shall become payable in full immediately and be paid by the Continuing Partners with interest at the Rate of Interest if the Continuing Partners:

(a) fail to comply with any provision of this deed;

(b) commit an act of bankruptcy; or

(c) die.

Part 7: Consequences of resignation or termination

(27) INDEMNITY

(i) The Continuing Partners shall (on the exercise of the option) covenant to discharge all the Partnership's liabilities and compensate the Seller in full on demand against all liabilities in respect of the Partnership.

(28) TAX ELECTION FOR CONTINUITY

(i) On the Relevant Event:

(b) the Seller shall if so requested by the Continuing Partners join with them in giving to HM Inspector of Taxes a notice; under the Income and Corporation Taxes Act 1988, s 113; and

(c) the Continuing Partners shall compensate the Seller in full on demand for any tax which is payable by him as a result of giving the notice in excess of the tax which would have been payable if no notice had been given.

(29) ATTORNEY ON RETIREMENT ETC

(i) Each Partner irrevocably appoints the Continuing Partners to be his attorney if he becomes a Seller to do anything and execute any document (at the sole cost and risk of the Continuing Partners) needed to:

  (b) carry on the Partnership business [so far as is necessary until it is wound up or transferred];

  (c) transfer his interest in the Partnership assets to the Continuing Partners; or

  (d) give notice of the change in the Partnership to its customers including the usual notice in the London Gazette.

Part 8: Administrative and general

(30) NOTICES

  (a) Any notice given under this deed shall be in writing and may be served:

    (a) personally;

    (b) by registered or recorded delivery mail;

    (c) by telex or facsimile transmission (the latter confirmed by telex or post); or

    (d) by any other means which any party specifies by notice to the others.

  (b) Each party's address for the service of notice shall be [his] above mentioned address or such other address as [he] specifies by notice to the others.

  (c) A notice shall be deemed to have been served:

    (a) if it was served in person, at the time of service;

    (b) if it was served by post, 48 hours after it was posted; and

    (c) if it was served by telex or facsimile transmission, at the time of transmission.

(31) ARBITRATION

(i) All disputes, differences and questions which at any time arise between the parties touching or arising out of or in connection with this deed or its subject matter shall be referred to a single arbitrator in accordance with the Arbitration Act 1996.

(32) INTERPRETATION

(a) Except where the context renders it absurd or impossible every reference to any party to this deed shall include his or her successors in title and personal representatives, by and against whom this agreement shall be enforceable as if they had been originally named as parties

(b) In this deed:

  (a) words expressed in any gender shall where the context so requires or permits include any other gender;

  (b) words importing persons shall include bodies corporate and partnerships and other incorporated bodies and vice versa;

  (c) words expressed in the singular shall where the context so requires or permits include the plural; and

  (d) where any party is more than one person:

    that party's obligations in this deed shall take effect as joint and several obligations;

    anything in this deed which applies to that party shall apply to all of those persons collectively and each of them separately; and

    the benefits contained in this deed in favour of that party shall take effect as conferred in favour of all of those persons collectively and each of them separately.

(c) The headings to clauses [and the table of clauses and marginal notes] are inserted for ease of reference only and shall not affect the construction of this deed.

(d) References in this deed to anything which any party is required to do or not to do shall include [his] acts, defaults and omissions, whether:

  (a) direct or indirect;

  (b) on his own account; or

  (c) for or through any other person; and

  (d) those which he permits or suffers to be done or not done by any other person.

(33) THIRD PARTIES

(i) Pursuant to s1(2)(a) of the Contracts (Rights of Third Parties) Act 1999 the parties intend that no terms of this deed may be enforced by a third party as defined in that Act.

SIGNED as a deed by [*name*] in the presence of

w   name   signature
i
t   Address
n
e
s
s   Occupation
etc for all the partners

Case-law summaries

Legal controls on partnerships:

A minor DOES have the capacity to become a partner and share in the profits but he cannot be personally sued for the firm's debts.
Lovell and Christmas v Beauchamp [1894]

A minor when he reaches 18, will still not become liable for his debts during his period of partnership as a minor. At 18 he can just carry on and automatically become a full partner but will not have to pay for his debts as a minor. Goode v Harrison [1821]

Restraint of trade clauses:

In Whitehill v Bradford [1952] a covenant not to carry on or concerned in carrying on the business or profession of medicine, surgery, midwifery or pharmacy or any branch thereof within 10 miles and for 21 years was upheld.

In Clarke v Newland [1991] the Court of Appeal upheld a clause which prohibited a partner in a general medical practice from practising within a defined area for 3 years after leaving the firm.

In Kaliszer v Ashley [2001] the court upheld a covenant which restricted an outgoing general practitioner from treating existing patients of the practice for 1 year within a radius of 3 miles.

In Dalles McMillan & Sinclair v Simpson [1989] the Court of Session held as UNREASONABLE a clause preventing a partner in a firm of solicitors in Glasgow from directly or indirectly carrying on business as a solicitor, except with the firm, within 20 miles of Glasgow Cross. This was because this area covered half the law firms in Scotland and this was unreasonable.

Restriction on choice of business names

In Ewing v Butterfield Margarine Co Ltd [1917], an injunction was had to stop a firm using a similar name and they were also awarded damages because it was found that the similar name was calculated to deceive and to divert business from the plaintiff to the defendant

General

Newstead v Frost [1980] 1 All ER 363 House of Lords,
The Inland Revenue attacked the partnership between David Frost and the Bahamian company. Mr Frost and the company formed a partnership to exploit "the activities of television and film consultants and advisors…and of producers, actors, directors, writers and artists." The Revenue tried to negative the partnership argued that a company cannot physically be a television entertainer or an author and so could not form a partnership for such purposes since the only other partner could not exploit his own skills. The House of Lords rejected this. There was nothing in the Partnership deed which required the company to entertain or write books and there was nothing to prevent the company and the individual jointly agreeing to exploit the individual's skills. A person can form a limited company and be the only director and can then also form a partnership with this limited company.

Moss v Elphick [1910] 1KB 846
A clause in the Partnership Deed made the partnership one for a fixed term. (see section 32(a) PA Act).

Law v Law [1905] 1 Ch 205
William Law and James Law were partners in a woollen manufacturer's business in Halifax, Yorkshire. William lived in London and took little part in the running of the business. James bought William's share of the business for

£21,000. Later, William discovered that the business was worth considerably more and that various assets unknown to him had not been disclosed. The Court of Appeal held that in principle this would allow William to set the contract aside.

(Section 28 PA Act—partners are bound to render TRUE ACCOUNTS and FULL INFORMATION of all things affecting the partnership at any partner or his legal representatives.

Moore v Moore [1998]

One partner in a farming business used funds, inter alia, to modernise his house.

Ward v Newalls Insulation Co.Ltd. [1998] LWLR 1722

Sleeping partners are well known by the Inland Revenue and are entitled to a share of the profits.

Highly v Walker [1910] 26 TLR 685

Powers of majority decision (section 24(8) PA Act). Three partners ran a profitable business. Two of the partners agreed to allow the son of one of them to be taken on as an apprentice to learn the business. The other partner objected and applied for an injunction. Judge Warrington decided that since the majority had acted properly, discussing the matter with the other partner, listening to his arguments and generally acting bona fide, their decision would stand. It was an ordinary matter connected with the partnership business within section 24(8) of the Partnership Act and thus a question for majority decision.

Popat v Schonchhatra [1997] 3 All ER 800 (CA)

There is a clear distinction between partnership capital on the one hand and partnership assets (or property) on the other. Partnership capital is the amount which each partner has agreed to contribute to the business, ie the total sum or investment in the business. So the partnership capital is a fixed sum. Partnership assets includes everything which belongs to the partnership.

In this case 2 partners contributed unequally to the business capital. The partnership was determined by the plaintiff and the defendant continued the business. Two and a half years later the defendant sold the business and realised a capital profit. In the ABSENCE OF ANY PARTNERSHIP DEED, the Court of Appeal held that after the partners had received their capital back, the surplus assets must be divided between them as being a profit under section 24(1) Partnership Act.

Dissolution of partnerships

Smith (petitioner) [1999]
In this case the insolvency applied both to the firm and at least one partner. The petitions were dealt with together.

Schooler v Customs & Excise Commissioners [1995]2BCLC 222
Mr & Mrs Schooler had been partners in a business which owed over £91,000.00 in unpaid VAT. The VAT authorities served statutory demands on both the partners for that amount. Failure to pay such a demand leads to a bankruptcy petition. Mr Schooner successfully negotiated an individual voluntary arrangement under the Insolvency Act 1986 in respect of his debts, including his liability for the VAT. The effect of this was to avoid the bankruptcy. Mrs Schooner failed to negotiate in one respect of her debts and so, having failed to pay, a bankruptcy order was made against her. She appealed to the Court of Appeal on the basis that no such order could be made against her without a concurrent petition to wind up the firm since both partners were jointly liable for the VAT debt.

The Court of Appeal dismissed this claim, principally because the 1986 Order, which applied in this case, expressly said that all partnership debts were also individual debts of each partner for the purposes of bringing a bankruptcy petition against a partner.

Oldham v Kyrris [1997]
The Kyrris family were partners in respect of several restaurants run on franchise agreements with Burger King and in premises sub-let from that well-known company.

Two of the Kyrris family were named on the leases. In 1996 the firm stopped paying Burger King royalties due under t5he franchise agreements and rent due under the sub-leases. Burger King brought an action against the two named partners for arrears of £1.63 million rent and £630,000 royalties. Those two partners counter-claimed against Burger King on various matters. In April 1997 The Royal Bank of Scotland successfully presented a petition for an administration order against the firm in respect of debts of £2.85 million. This was because this was a better way of realising the assets than a winding-up.

The administrators concluded that if the business was sold as a going concern it would raise £6 million and so pay off all the creditors. But to do that they needed the consent of Burger King who could end the sub-leases and the franchise agreements, thus destroying at one stroke the value of the partnership business. Burger King was willing to cooperate only if the overall settlement included the claims brought against the company by the two partners, who did not wish this to happen. So the administrators asked the court whether they could in effect take over that counterclaim as part of the administration. Judge Evans-Lombe, held first that the counterclaim was a partnership asset. Any sums recovered would accrue to the firm and not just the two partners. He then said that the position of an administrator of a partnership was like that f an administrator appointed over the assets of a company. On that basis, partnership assets, even those held in the name of individual partners, were under the control of the administrators to dispose of as they wished for the purpose of the administration.

Insolvent Partnerships

Re West Park Golf & Country Club [1997] 1 BCLC 20

A petition was struck out where the partners presenting the petition had failed to disclose in their supporting affidavit the fact that there was a substantial secured creditor, the bank, which had not been consulted. The petition had been presented for the sole purpose of frustrating the bank in realising its security.

Re Greek Taverna [1999] BCC 153

The Court, in making an administration order, must be satisfied that it will be likely to achieve one or more purposes laid down in the Order.
This partnership had been formed in 1992 between Mr Harper and Mr Cotsicoros who had fallen out and so never met to discuss the business. The firm became overdrawn by £17,000 and Mrs Harper owed the bank a further £8,000. Mrs Harper petitioned for an administration order. The partnership was also owing rent. The petition proposed that Mr Rout, an insolvency practitioner, be appointed as administrator.
Mr Rout drew up a report which indicated that the partnership was insolvent and that if it were wound up, with a forced sale of the business, it would produce a deficit of £68,000, ignoring the cost of the winding up. But if an administration order were made, however, the business could be sold as a going concern which would produce an estimated surplus of £3,000. Furthermore there would be an estimated profit of £9,000 if the business continued for six

weeks before the sale. The petition was opposed by Mr Cotsicoros but this was dismissed by the judge. The judge said, "It does seem to me on the evidence that the alternative to an administration order is an imminent winding up of the partnership as an insolvent partnership...It seems to me that the evidence does establish that the making of an administration order will be likely to result in a more advantageous realisation of the partnership property than would be effected in the winding up..."

Partnership Act 1890

1890 Chapter 39
An Act to declare and amend the Law of Partnership
(14th August 1890)

Nature of Partnership

1   Definition of Partnership

(1) Partnership is the relation which subsists between persons carrying on a business in common with a view of profit.

(2) But the relation between members of any company or association which is—

   (a) Registered as a Company under the Companies Act 1862 or any other Act of Parliament for the time being in force and relating to the registration of joint stock companies; or

   (b) Formed or incorporated by or in pursuance of any other Act of Parliament or letters patent, or Royal Charter.

   (c) ...:

is not a partnership within the meaning of this Act.

2   Rules for determining existence of partnership

In determining whether a partnership does or does not exist, regard shall be had to the following rules:

   (1) Joint tenancy, tenancy in common, joint property, common property, or part ownership does not of itself create a partnership as to anything so held or owned, whether the tenants or owners do or do not share any profits made by the use thereof.

(2) The sharing of gross returns does not of itself create a partnership, whether the persons sharing such returns have or have not a joint or common right or interest in any property from which or from the use of which the returns are derived.

(3) The receipt by a person of a share of the profits of a business is prima facie evidence that he is a partner in the business, but receipt of such a share, or of a payment contingent on or varying with the profits of a business, does not of itself make him a partner in the business; and in particular—

   (a) The receipt by a person of a debt or other liquidated amount by instalments or otherwise out of the accruing profits of a business does not of itself make him a partner in the business or liable as such:

   (b) A contract for the remuneration of a servant or agent of a person engaged in a business by a share of the profits of the business does not of itself make the servant or agent a partner in the business or liable as such:

   (c) A person being the widow or child of a deceased partner, and receiving by way of annuity a portion of the profits made in the business in which the deceased person was a partner, is not by reason only of such receipt a partner in the business or liable as such:

   (d) The advance of money by way of loan to a person engaged or about to engage in any business on a contract with that person that the lender shall receive a rate of interest varying with the profits, or shall receive a share of the profits arising from carrying on the business, does not of itself make the lender a partner with the person or persons carrying on the business or liable as such. Provided that the contract is in writing, and signed by or on behalf of all the parties thereto:

   (e) A person receiving by way of annuity or otherwise a portion of the profits of a business in consideration of the sale by him of the goodwill of the business is not by reason only of such receipt a partner in the business or liable as such.

3 Postponement of rights of person lending or selling in consideration of share of profits in case of insolvency

In the event of any person to whom money has been advanced by way of loan upon such a contract as is mentioned in the last foregoing section, or of any buyer of a goodwill in consideration of a share of the profits of the business, being adjudged a bankrupt, entering into an arrangement to pay his creditors less than 100p in the pound, or dying in insolvent circumstances, the lender of the loan shall not be entitled to recover anything in respect of his loan, and the seller of the goodwill shall not be entitled to recover anything in respect of the share of profits contracted for, until the claims of the other creditors of the borrower or buyer for valuable consideration in money or money's worth have been satisfied.

4   Meaning of firm

(1) Persons who have entered into partnership with one another are for the purposes of this Act called collectively a firm, and the name under which their business is carried on is called the firm-name.

(2) In Scotland a firm is a legal person distinct from the partners of whom it is composed, but an individual partner may be charged on a decree or diligence directed against the firm, and on payment of the debts is entitled to relief pro rata from the firm and its other members.

Relations of Partners to persons dealing with them

5   Power of partner to bind the firm

Every partner is an agent of the firm and his other partners for the purpose of the business of the partnership; and the acts of every partner who does any act for carrying on in the usual way business of the kind carried on by the firm of which he is a member bind the firm and his partners, unless the partner so acting has in fact no authority to act for the firm in the particular matter, and the person with whom he is dealing either knows that he has no authority, or does not know or believe him to be a partner.

6   Partners bound by acts on behalf of firm

An act or instrument relating to the business of the firm done or executed in the firm-name, or in any other manner showing an intention to bind the firm, by any person thereto authorised, whether a partner or not, is binding on the firm and all the partners.

Provided that this section shall not affect any general rule of law relating to the execution of deeds or negotiable instruments.

7 Partner using credit of firm for private purposes

Where one partner pledges the credit of the firm for a purpose apparently not connected with the firm's ordinary course of business, the firm is not bound, unless he is in fact specially authorised by the other partners; but this section does not affect any personal liability incurred by an individual partner.

8 Effect of notice that firm will not be bound by acts of partner

If it has been agreed between the partners that any restriction shall be placed on the power of any one or more of them to bind the firm, no act done in contravention of the agreement is binding on the firm with respect to persons having notice of the agreement.

9 Liability of partners

Every partner in a firm is liable jointly with the other partners, and in Scotland severally also, for all debts and obligations of the firm incurred while he is a partner; and after his death his estate is also severally liable in a due course of administration for such debts and obligations, so far as they remain unsatisfied, but subject in England or Ireland to the prior payment of his separate debts.

10 Liability of the firm for wrongs

Where, by any wrongful act or omission of any partner acting in the ordinary course of the business of the firm, or with the authority of his co-partners, loss or injury is caused to any person not being a partner in the firm, or any penalty is incurred, the firm is liable therefor to the same extent as the partner so acting or omitting to act.

11 Misapplication of money or property received for or in custody of the firm

In the following cases; namely—

(a) Where one partner acting within the scope of his apparent authority receives the money or property of a third person and misapplies it; and

(b) Where a firm in the course of its business receives money or property of a third person, and the money or property so received is misapplied by one or more of the partners while it is in the custody of the firm;

the firm is liable to make good the loss.

12 Liability for wrongs joint and several

Every partner is liable jointly with his co-partners and also severally for everything for which the firm while he is a partner therein becomes liable under either of the two last preceding sections.

13 Improper employment of trust-property for partnership purposes

If a partner, being a trustee, improperly employs trust-property in the business or on the account of the partnership, no other partner is liable for the trust property to the persons beneficially interested therein:
Provided as follows:—

(1) This section shall not affect any liability incurred by any partner by reason of his having notice of a breach of trust; and

(2) Nothing in this section shall prevent trust money from being followed and recovered from the firm if still in its possession or under its control.

14 Persons liable by "holding out"

(1) Every one who by words spoken or written or by conduct represents himself, or who knowingly suffers himself to be represented, as a partner in a particular firm, is liable as a partner to any one who has on the faith of any such representation given credit to the firm, whether the representation has or has not been made or communicated to the person so giving credit by or with the knowledge of the apparent partner making the representation or suffering it to be made.

(2) Provided that where after a partner's death the partnership business is continued in the old firm's name, the continued use of that name or of the deceased partner's name as part thereof shall not of itself make his executors or administrators estate or effects liable for any partnership debts contracted after his death.

15 Admissions and representation of partners

An admission or representation made by any partner concerning the partnership affairs, and in the ordinary course of its business, is evidence against the firm.

16   Notice to acting partner to be notice to the firm

Notice to any partner who habitually acts in the partnership business of any matter relating to partnership affairs operates as notice to the firm, except in the case of a fraud on the firm committed by or with the consent of that partner.

17   Liabilities of incoming and outgoing partners

(1) A person who is admitted as a partner into an existing firm does not thereby become liable to the creditors of the firm for anything done before he became a partner.

(2) A partner who retires from a firm does not thereby cease to be liable for partnership debts or obligations incurred before his retirement.

(3) A retiring partner may be discharged from any existing liabilities, by an agreement to that effect between himself and the members of the firm as newly constituted and the creditors, and this agreement may be either expressed or inferred as a fact from the course of dealing between the creditors and the firm as newly constituted.

18   Revocation of continuing guaranty by change in firm

A continuing guaranty or cautionary obligation given either to a firm or to a third person in respect of the transactions of a firm is, in the absence of agreement to the contrary, revoked as to future transactions by any change in the constitution of the firm to which, or of the firm in respect of the transactions of which, the guaranty or obligation was given.

Relations of Partners to one another

19   Variation by consent of terms of partnership

The mutual rights and duties of partners, whether ascertained by agreement or defined by this Act, may be varied by the consent of all the partners, and such consent may be either express or inferred from a course of dealing.

20   Partnership property

(1) All property and rights and interests in property originally brought into the partnership stock or acquired, whether by purchase or otherwise, on account of the firm, or for the purposes and in the course of the partnership business, are called in this Act partnership property, and must be held

and applied by the partners exclusively for the purposes of the partnership and in accordance with the partnership agreement.

(2) Provided that the legal estate or interest in any land, or in Scotland the title to and interest in any heritable estate, which belongs to the partnership shall devolve according to the nature and tenure thereof, and the general rules of law thereto applicable, but in trust, so far as necessary, for the persons beneficially interested in the land under this section.

(3) Where co-owners of an estate or interest in any land, or in Scotland of any heritable estate, not being itself partnership property, are partners as to profits made by the use of that land or estate, and purchase other land or estate out of the profits to be used in like manner, the land or estate so purchased belongs to them, in the absence of an agreement to the contrary, not as partners, but as co-owners for the same respective estates and interests as are held by them in the land or estate first mentioned at the date of the purchase.

21 Property bought with partnership money

Unless the contrary intention appears, property bought with money belonging to the firm is deemed to have been bought on account of the firm.

22 ...

23 Procedure against partnership property for a partner's separate judgement debt

(1) ...A writ of execution shall not issue against any partnership property except on a judgment against the firm.

(2) The High Court, or a judge thereof,..., or a county court, may, on the application by summons of any judgment creditor of a partner, make an order charging that partner's interest in the partnership property and profits with payment of the amount of the judgment debt and interest thereon, and may by the same or a subsequent order appoint a receiver of that partner's share of profits (whether already declared or accruing), and of any other money which may be coming to him in respect of the partnership, and direct all accounts and inquiries, and give all other orders and directions which might have been directed or given if the charge had been made in favour of the judgment creditor by the partner, or which the circumstances of the case may require.

(3) The other partner or partners shall be at liberty at any time to redeem the interest charged, or in case of a sale being directed, to purchase the same.

(4) ...

(5) This section shall not apply to Scotland.

24   Rules as to interests and duties of partners subject to special agreement

The interests of partners in the partnership property and their rights and duties in relation to the partnership shall be determined, subject to any agreement express or implied between the partners, by the following rules:—

(1) All the partners are entitled to share equally in the capital and profits of the business, and must contribute equally towards the losses whether of capital or otherwise sustained by the firm.

(2) The firm must indemnify every partner in respect of payments made and personal liabilities incurred by him—

(a) In the ordinary and proper conduct of the business of the firm; or,

(b) In or about anything necessarily done for the preservation of the business or property of the firm.

(3) A partner making, for the purpose of the partnership, any actual payment or advance beyond the amount of capital which he has agreed to subscribe, is entitled to interest at the rate of five per cent. per annum from the date of the payment or advance.

(4) A partner is not entitled, before the ascertainment of profits, to interest on the capital subscribed by him.

(5) Every partner may take part in the management of the partnership business.

(6) No partner shall be entitled to remuneration for acting in the partnership business.

(7) No person may be introduced as a partner without the consent of all existing partners.

(8) Any difference arising as to ordinary matters connected with the partnership business may be decided by a majority of the partners, but no change may be made in the nature of the partnership business without the consent of all existing partners.

(9) The partnership books are to be kept at the place of business of the partnership (or the principal place, if there is more than one), and

every partner may, when he thinks fit, have access to and inspect and copy any of them.

25 Expulsion of partner

No majority of the partners can expel any partner unless a power to do so has been conferred by express agreement between the partners.

26 Retirement from partnership at will

(1) Where no fixed term has been agreed upon for the duration of the partnership, any partner may determine the partnership at any time on giving notice of his intention so to do to all the other partners.

(2) Where the partnership has originally been constituted by deed, a notice in writing, signed by the partner giving it, shall be sufficient for this purpose.

27 Where partnership for term is continued over, continuance on old terms presumed

(1) Where a partnership entered into for a fixed term is continued after the term has expired, and without any express new agreement, the rights and duties of the partners remain the same as they were at the expiration of the term, so far as is consistent with the incidents of a partnership at will.

(2) A continuance of the business by the partners or such of them as habitually acted therein during the term, without any settlement or liquidation of the partnership affairs, is presumed to be a continuance of the partnership.

28 Duty of partners to render accounts, etc

Partners are bound to render true accounts and full information of all things affecting the partnership to any partner or his legal representatives.

29 Accountability of partners for private profits

(1) Every partner must account to the firm for any benefit derived by him without the consent of the other partners from any transaction concerning the partnership, or from any use by him of the partnership property name or business connection.

(2) This section applies also to transactions undertaken after a partnership has been dissolved by the death of a partner, and before the affairs thereof have

been completely wound up, either by any surviving partner or by the representatives of the deceased partner.

30 Duty of partner not to compete with firm

If a partner, without the consent of the other partners, carries on any business of the same nature as and competing with that of the firm, he must account for and pay over to the firm all profits made by him in that business.

31 Rights of assignee of share in partnership

(1) An assignment by any partner of his share in the partnership, either absolute or by way of mortgage or redeemable charge, does not, as against the other partners, entitle the assignee, during the continuance of the partnership, to interfere in the management or administration of the partnership business or affairs, or to require any accounts of the partnership transactions, or to inspect the partnership books, but entitles the assignee only to receive the share of profits to which the assigning partner would otherwise be entitled, and the assignee must accept the account of profits agreed to by the partners.

(2) In case of a dissolution of the partnership, whether as respects all the partners or as respects the assigning partner, the assignee is entitled to receive the share of the partnership assets to which the assigning partner is entitled as between himself and the other partners, and, for the purpose of ascertaining that share, to an account as from the date of the dissolution.

Dissolution of Partnership, and its consequences

32 Dissolution by expiration or notice

Subject to any agreement between the partners, a partnership is dissolved—

    (a) If entered into for a fixed term, by the expiration of that term:

    (b) If entered into for a single adventure or undertaking, by the termination of that adventure or undertaking:

    (c) If entered into for an undefined time, by any partner giving notice to the other or others of his intention to dissolve the partnership.

In the last-mentioned case the partnership is dissolved as from the date mentioned in the notice as the date of dissolution, or, if no date is so mentioned, as from the date of the communication of the notice.

33 Dissolution by bankruptcy, death or charge

(1) Subject to any agreement between the partners, every partnership is dissolved as regards all the partners by the death or bankruptcy of any partner.

(2) A partnership may, at the option of the other partners, be dissolved if any partner suffers his share of the partnership property to be charged under this Act for his separate debt.

34 Dissolution by illegality of partnership

A partnership is in every case dissolved by the happening of any event which makes it unlawful for the business of the firm to be carried on or for the members of the firm to carry it on in partnership.

35 Dissolution by the Court

On application by a partner the Court may decree a dissolution of the partnership in any of the following cases:

    (a) ...

    (b) When a partner, other than the partner suing, becomes in any other way permanently incapable of performing his part of the partnership contract:

    (c) When a partner, other than the partner suing, has been guilty of such conduct as, in the opinion of the Court, regard being had to the nature of the business, is calculated to prejudicially affect the carrying on of the business:

    (d) When a partner, other than the partner suing, wilfully or persistently commits a breach of the partnership agreement, or otherwise so conducts himself in matters relating to the partnership business that it is not reasonably practicable for the other partner or partners to carry on the business in partnership with him:

    (e) When the business of the partnership can only be carried on at a loss:

    (f) Whenever in any case circumstances have arisen which, in the opinion of the Court, render it just and equitable that the partnership be dissolved.

36 Rights of persons dealing with firm against apparent members of firm

(1) Where a person deals with a firm after a change in its constitution he is entitled to treat all apparent members of the old firm as still being members of the firm until he has notice of the change.

(2) An advertisement in the London Gazette as to a firm whose principal place of business is in England or Wales, in the Edinburgh Gazette as to a firm whose principal place of business is in Scotland, and in the [Belfast] Gazette as to a firm whose principal place of business is in Ireland, shall be notice as to persons who had not dealings with the firm before the date of the dissolution or change so advertised.

(3) The estate of a partner who dies, or who becomes bankrupt, or of a partner who, not having been known to the person dealing with the firm to be a partner, retires from the firm, is not liable for partnership debts contracted after the date of the death, bankruptcy, or retirement respectively.

37 Right of partners to notify dissolution

On the dissolution of a partnership or retirement of a partner any partner may publicly notify the same, and may require the other partner or partners to concur for that purpose in all necessary or proper acts, if any, which cannot be done without his or their concurrence.

38 Continuing authority of partners for purposes of winding up

After the dissolution of a partnership the authority of each partner to bind the firm, and the other rights and obligations of the partners, continue notwithstanding the dissolution so far as may be necessary to wind up the affairs of the partnership, and to complete transactions begun but unfinished at the time of the dissolution, but not otherwise.

Provided that the firm is in no case bound by the acts of a partner who has become bankrupt; but this proviso does not affect the liability of any person who has after the bankruptcy represented himself or knowingly suffered himself to be represented as a partner of the bankrupt.

39 Rights of partners as to application of partnership property

On the dissolution of a partnership every partner is entitled, as against the other partners in the firm, and all persons claiming through them in respect of their interests as partners, to have the property of the partnership applied in payment of the debts and liabilities of the firm, and to have the surplus assets after such payment applied in payment of what may be due to the partners respectively after deducting what may be due from them as partners to the firm; and for that purpose any partner or his representatives may on the termination of the partnership apply to the Court to wind up the business and affairs of the firm.

40 Apportionment of premium where partnership prematurely dissolved

Where one partner has paid a premium to another on entering into a partnership for a fixed term, and the partnership is dissolved before the expiration of that term otherwise than by the death of a partner, the Court may order the repayment of the premium, or of such part thereof as it thinks just, having regard to the terms of the partnership contract and to the length of time during which the partnership has continued; unless

(a) the dissolution is, in the judgment of the Court, wholly or chiefly due to the misconduct of the partner who paid the premium; or

(b) the partnership has been dissolved by an agreement containing no provision for a return of any part of the premium.

41 Rights where partnership dissolved for fraud or misrepresentation

Where a partnership contract is rescinded on the ground of the fraud or misrepresentation of one of the parties thereto, the party entitled to rescind is, without prejudice to any other right, entitled—

(a) to a lien on, or right of retention of, the surplus of the partnership assets, after satisfying the partnership liabilities, for any sum of money paid by him for the purchase of a share in the partnership and for any capital contributed by him, and is

(b) to stand in the place of the creditors of the firm for any payments made by him in respect of the partnership liabilities, and

(c) to be indemnified by the person guilty of the fraud or making the representation against all the debts and liabilities of the firm.

42 Right of outgoing partner in certain cases to share profits made after dissolution

(1) Where any member of a firm has died or otherwise ceased to be a partner, and the surviving or continuing partners carry on the business of the firm with its capital or assets without any final settlement of accounts as between the firm and the outgoing partner or his estate, then, in the

absence of any agreement to the contrary, the outgoing partner or his estate is entitled at the option of himself or his representatives to such share of the profits made since the dissolution as the Court may find to be attributable to the use of his share of the partnership assets, or to interest at the rate of five per cent. per annum on the amount of his share of the partnership assets.

(2) Provided that where by the partnership contract an option is given to surviving or continuing partners to purchase the interest of a deceased or outgoing partner, and that option is duly exercised, the estate of the deceased partner, or the outgoing partner or his estate, as the case may be, is not entitled to any further or other share of profits; but if any partner assuming to act in exercise of the option does not in all material respects comply with the terms thereof, he is liable to account under the foregoing provisions of this section.

43   Retiring or deceased partner's share to be a debt

Subject to any agreement between the partners, the amount due from surviving or continuing partners to an outgoing partner or the representatives of a deceased partner in respect of the outgoing or deceased partner's share is a debt accruing at the date of the dissolution or death.

44   Rule for distribution of assets on final settlement of accounts

In settling accounts between the partners after a dissolution of partnership, the following rules shall, subject to any agreement, be observed:

(a) Losses, including losses and deficiencies of capital, shall be paid first out of profits, next out of capital, and lastly, if necessary, by the partners individually in the proportion in which they were entitled to share profits:

(b) The assets of the firm including the sums, if any, contributed by the partners to make up losses or deficiencies of capital, shall be applied in the following manner and order:

1   In paying the debts and liabilities of the firm to persons who are not partners therein:

2   In paying to each partner rateably what is due from the firm to him for advances as distinguished from capital:

3   In paying to each partner rateably what is due from the firm to him in respect of capital:

4 The ultimate residue, if any, shall be divided among the partners in the proportion in which profits are divisible.

Supplemental

45 Definitions of "court" and "business"

In this Act, unless the contrary intention appears,—

The expression "court" includes every court and judge having jurisdiction in the case:

The expression "business" includes every trade, occupation, or profession.

46 Saving for rules of equity and common law

The rules of equity and of common law applicable to partnership shall continue in force except so far as they are inconsistent with the express provisions of this Act.

Limited Liability Partnerships Act 2000

Introduction

1 Limited liability partnerships

(1) There shall be a new form of legal entity to be known as a limited liability partnership.

(2) A limited liability partnership is a body corporate (with legal personality separate from that of its members) which is formed by being incorporated under this Act; and—

(a) in the following provisions of this Act (except in the phrase "oversea limited liability partnership"), and

(b) in any other enactment (except where provision is made to the contrary or the context otherwise requires),

references to a limited liability partnership are to such a body corporate.

(3) A limited liability partnership has unlimited capacity.

(4) The members of a limited liability partnership have such liability to contribute to its assets in the event of its being wound up as is provided for by virtue of this Act.

(5) Accordingly, except as far as otherwise provided by this Act or any other enactment, the law relating to partnerships does not apply to a limited liability partnership.

(6) The Schedule (which makes provision about the names and registered offices of limited liability partnerships) has effect.

Incorporation

2   Incorporation document etc

(1) For a limited liability partnership to be incorporated—

(a) two or more persons associated for carrying on a lawful business with a view to profit must have subscribed their names to an incorporation document,

(b) there must have been delivered to the registrar either the incorporation document or a copy authenticated in a manner approved by him, and

(c) there must have been so delivered a statement in a form approved by the registrar, made by either a solicitor engaged in the formation of the limited liability partnership or anyone who subscribed his name to the incorporation document, that the requirement imposed by paragraph (a) has been complied with.

(2) The incorporation document must—

(a) be in a form approved by the registrar (or as near to such a form as circumstances allow),

(b) state the name of the limited liability partnership,

(c) state whether the registered office of the limited liability partnership is to be situated in England and Wales, in Wales or in Scotland,

(d) state the address of that registered office,

(e) state the name and address of each of the persons who are to be members of the limited liability partnership on incorporation, and

(f) either specify which of those persons are to be designated members or state that every person who from time to time is a member of the limited liability partnership is a designated member.

(2A) Where a confidentiality order, made under section 723B of the Companies Act 1985 as applied to a limited liability partnerships, is in force in respect of any individual named as a member of a limited liability partnership under subsection (2) that subsection shall have effect as if the reference to the address of the individual were a reference to the address for the time being notified by him under the Limited Liability Partnerships (Particulars of Usual Residential Address) (Confidentiality Orders) Regulations 2002 to any limited liability partnership of which he is a member or if he is not such a member either the address specified in his application for a confidentiality order or the address last notified by him under such a confidentiality order as the case may be.

(2B) Where the incorporation document or a copy of such delivered under this section includes an address specified in reliance on subsection (2A) there shall be delivered with it or the copy of it a statement in a form approved by the registrar containing particulars of the usual residential address of the member whose address is so specified.

(3) If a person makes a false statement under subsection (1)(c) which he—

(a) knows to be false, or

(b) does not believe to be true,

he commits an offence.

(4) A person guilty of an offence under subsection (3) is liable—

(a) on summary conviction, to imprisonment for a period not exceeding six months or a fine not exceeding the statutory maximum, or to both, or

(b) on conviction on indictment, to imprisonment for a period not exceeding two years or a fine, or to both.

3   Incorporation by registration

(1) When the requirements imposed by paragraphs (b) and (c) of subsection (1) of section 2 have been complied with, the registrar shall retain the incorporation document or copy delivered to him and, unless the requirement imposed by paragraph (a) of that subsection has not been complied with, he shall—

(a) register the incorporation document or copy, and

(b) give a certificate that the limited liability partnership is incorporated by the name specified in the incorporation document.

(2) The registrar may accept the statement delivered under paragraph (c) of subsection (1) of section 2 as sufficient evidence that the requirement imposed by paragraph (a) of that subsection has been complied with.

(3) The certificate shall either be signed by the registrar or be authenticated by his official seal.

(4) The certificate is conclusive evidence that the requirements of section 2 are complied with and that the limited liability partnership is incorporated by the name specified in the incorporation document.

Membership

4   Members

(1) On the incorporation of a limited liability partnership its members are the persons who subscribed their names to the incorporation document (other than any who have died or been dissolved).

(2) Any other person may become a member of a limited liability partnership by and in accordance with an agreement with the existing members.

(3) A person may cease to be a member of a limited liability partnership (as well as by death or dissolution) in accordance with an agreement with the other members or, in the absence of agreement with the other members as to cessation of membership, by giving reasonable notice to the other members.

(4) A member of a limited liability partnership shall not be regarded for any purpose as employed by the limited liability partnership unless, if he and the other members were partners in a partnership, he would be regarded for that purpose as employed by the partnership.

5   Relationship of members etc

(1) Except as far as otherwise provided by this Act or any other enactment, the mutual rights and duties of the members of a limited liability partnership, and the mutual rights and duties of a limited liability partnership and its members, shall be governed—

(a) by agreement between the members, or between the limited liability partnership and its members, or

(b) in the absence of agreement as to any matter, by any provision made in relation to that matter by regulations under section 15(c).

(2) An agreement made before the incorporation of a limited liability partnership between the persons who subscribe their names to the incorporation document may impose obligations on the limited liability partnership (to take effect at any time after its incorporation).

6   Members as agents

(1) Every member of a limited liability partnership is the agent of the limited liability partnership.

(2) But a limited liability partnership is not bound by anything done by a member in dealing with a person if—

(a) the member in fact has no authority to act for the limited liability partnership by doing that thing, and

(b) the person knows that he has no authority or does not know or believe him to be a member of the limited liability partnership.

(3) Where a person has ceased to be a member of a limited liability partnership, the former member is to be regarded (in relation to any person dealing with the limited liability partnership) as still being a member of the limited liability partnership unless—

(a) the person has notice that the former member has ceased to be a member of the limited liability partnership, or

(b) notice that the former member has ceased to be a member of the limited liability partnership has been delivered to the registrar.

(4) Where a member of a limited liability partnership is liable to any person (other than another member of the limited liability partnership) as a result of a wrongful act or omission of his in the course of the business of the limited liability partnership or with its authority, the limited liability partnership is liable to the same extent as the member.

7   Ex-members

(1) This section applies where a member of a limited liability partnership has either ceased to be a member or—

(a) has died,

(b) has become bankrupt or had his estate sequestrated or has been wound up,

(c) has granted a trust deed for the benefit of his creditors, or

(d) has assigned the whole or any part of his share in the limited liability partnership (absolutely or by way of charge or security).

(2) In such an event the former member or—

(a) his personal representative,

(b) his trustee in bankruptcy or permanent or interim trustee (within the meaning of the Bankruptcy (Scotland) Act 1985) or liquidator,

(c) his trustee under the trust deed for the benefit of his creditors, or

(d) his assignee,

may not interfere in the management or administration of any business or affairs of the limited liability partnership.

(3) But subsection (2) does not affect any right to receive an amount from the limited liability partnership in that event.

8   Designated members

(1) If the incorporation document specifies who are to be designated members—

(a) they are designated members on incorporation, and

(b) any member may become a designated member by and in accordance with an agreement with the other members,

and a member may cease to be a designated member in accordance with an agreement with the other members.

(2) But if there would otherwise be no designated members, or only one, every member is a designated member.

(3) If the incorporation document states that every person who from time to time is a member of the limited liability partnership is a designated member, every member is a designated member.

(4) A limited liability partnership may at any time deliver to the registrar—

(a) notice that specified members are to be designated members, or

(b) notice that every person who from time to time is a member of the limited liability partnership is a designated member,

and, once it is delivered, subsection (1) (apart from paragraph (a)) and subsection (2), or subsection (3), shall have effect as if that were stated in the incorporation document.

(5) A notice delivered under subsection (4)—

(a) shall be in a form approved by the registrar, and

(b) shall be signed by a designated member of the limited liability partnership or authenticated in a manner approved by the registrar.

(6) A person ceases to be a designated member if he ceases to be a member.

9   Registration of membership changes

(1)   A limited liability partnership must ensure that—

(a)   where a person becomes or ceases to be a member or designated member, notice is delivered to the registrar within fourteen days, and

(b)   where there is any change in the name or address of a member, notice is delivered to the registrar within 28 days.

(2)   Where all the members from time to time of a limited liability partnership are designated members, subsection (1)(a) does not require notice that a person has become or ceased to be a designated member as well as a member.

(3)   A notice delivered under subsection (1)—

(a)   shall be in a form approved by the registrar, and

(b)   shall be signed by a designated member of the limited liability partnership or authenticated in a manner approved by the registrar,

and, if it relates to a person becoming a member or designated member, shall contain a statement that he consents to becoming a member or designated member signed by him or authenticated in a manner approved by the registrar.

(3A) Where a confidentiality order under section 723B of the Companies Act 1985 as applied to limited liability partnerships is made in respect of an existing member, the limited liability partnership must ensure that there is delivered within 28 days to the registrar notice in a form approved by the registrar containing the address for the time being notified to it by the member under the Limited Liability Partnerships (Particulars of Usual Residential Address) (Confidentiality Orders) Regulations 2002.

(3B) Where such a confidentiality order is in force in respect of a member the requirement in subsection (1)(b) to notify a change in the address of a member shall be read in relation to that member as a requirement to deliver to the registrar, within 28 days, notice of—

(a)   any change in the usual residential address of that member; and

(b)   any change in the address for the time being notified to the limited liability partnership by the member under the Limited Liability Partnerships (Particulars of Usual Residential Address) (Confidentiality Orders) Regulations 2002, and the registrar may approve different forms for the notification of each kind of address.

(4) If a limited liability partnership fails to comply with subsection (1), the partnership and every designated member commits an offence.

(5) But it is a defence for a designated member charged with an offence under subsection (4) to prove that he took all reasonable steps for securing that subsection (1) was complied with.

(6) A person guilty of an offence under subsection (4) is liable on summary conviction to a fine not exceeding level 5 on the standard scale.

Taxation

10   Income tax and chargeable gains

(1) In the Income and Corporation Taxes Act 1988, after section 118 insert—

"Limited liability partnerships

118ZA Treatment of limited liability partnerships

For the purposes of the Tax Acts, a trade, profession or business carried on by a limited liability partnership with a view to profit shall be treated as carried on in partnership by its members (and not by the limited liability partnership as such); and, accordingly, the property of the limited liability partnership shall be treated for those purposes as partnership property.

118ZB Restriction on relief

Sections 117 and 118 have effect in relation to a member of a limited liability partnership as in relation to a limited partner, but subject to sections 118ZC and 118ZD.

118ZC Member's contribution to trade

(1) Subsection (3) of section 117 does not have effect in relation to a member of a limited liability partnership.

(2) But, for the purposes of that section and section 118, such a member's contribution to a trade at any time ("the relevant time") is the greater of—

(a) the amount subscribed by him, and

(b) the amount of his liability on a winding up.

(3) The amount subscribed by a member of a limited liability partnership is the amount which he has contributed to the limited liability partnership as capital, less so much of that amount (if any) as—

(a) he has previously, directly or indirectly, drawn out or received back,

(b) he so draws out or receives back during the period of five years beginning with the relevant time,

(c) he is or may be entitled so to draw out or receive back at any time when he is a member of the limited liability partnership, or

(d) he is or may be entitled to require another person to reimburse to him.

(4) The amount of the liability of a member of a limited liability partnership on a winding up is the amount which—

(a) he is liable to contribute to the assets of the limited liability partnership in the event of its being wound up, and

(b) he remains liable so to contribute for the period of at least five years beginning with the relevant time (or until it is wound up, if that happens before the end of that period).

118ZD Carry forward of unrelieved losses

(1) Where amounts relating to a trade carried on by a member of a limited liability partnership are, in any one or more chargeable periods, prevented from being given or allowed by section 117 or 118 as it applies otherwise than by virtue of this section (his "total unrelieved loss"), subsection (2) applies in each subsequent chargeable period in which—

(a) he carries on the trade as a member of the limited liability partnership, and

(b) any of his total unrelieved loss remains outstanding.

(2) Sections 380, 381, 393A(1) and 403 (and sections 117 and 118 as they apply in relation to those sections) shall have effect in the subsequent chargeable period as if—

(a) any loss sustained or incurred by the member in the trade in that chargeable period were increased by an amount equal to so much of his total unrelieved loss as remains outstanding in that period, or

(b) (if no loss is so sustained or incurred) a loss of that amount were so sustained or incurred.

(3) To ascertain whether any (and, if so, how much) of a member's total unrelieved loss remains outstanding in the subsequent chargeable period, deduct from the amount of his total unrelieved loss the aggregate of—

(a) any relief given under any provision of the Tax Acts (otherwise than as a result of subsection (2)) in respect of his total unrelieved loss in that or any previous chargeable period, and

(b) any amount given or allowed in respect of his total unrelieved loss as a result of subsection (2) in any previous chargeable period (or which would have been so given or allowed had a claim been made)."

(2) In section 362(2)(a) of that Act (loan to buy into partnership), after "partner" insert "in a limited partnership registered under the Limited Partnerships Act 1907".

(3) In the Taxation of Chargeable Gains Act 1992, after section 59 insert—

"59A Limited liability partnerships

(1) Where a limited liability partnership carries on a trade or business with a view to profit—

(a) assets held by the limited liability partnership shall be treated for the purposes of tax in respect of chargeable gains as held by its members as partners, and

(b) any dealings by the limited liability partnership shall be treated for those purposes as dealings by its members in partnership (and not by the limited liability partnership as such),

and tax in respect of chargeable gains accruing to the members of the limited liability partnership on the disposal of any of its assets shall be assessed and charged on them separately.

(2) Where subsection (1) ceases to apply in relation to a limited liability partnership with the effect that tax is assessed and charged—

(a) on the limited liability partnership (as a company) in respect of chargeable gains accruing on the disposal of any of its assets, and

(b) on the members in respect of chargeable gains accruing on the disposal of any of their capital interests in the limited liability partnership,

it shall be assessed and charged on the limited liability partnership as if subsection (1) had never applied in relation to it.

(3) Neither the commencement of the application of subsection (1) nor the cessation of its application in relation to a limited liability partnership is

to be taken as giving rise to the disposal of any assets by it or any of its members."

(4) After section 156 of that Act insert—

"156A Cessation of trade by limited liability partnership

(1) Where, immediately before the time of cessation of trade, a member of a limited liability partnership holds an asset, or an interest in an asset, acquired by him for a consideration treated as reduced under section 152 or 153, he shall be treated as if a chargeable gain equal to the amount of the reduction accrued to him immediately before that time.

(2) Where, as a result of section 154(2), a chargeable gain on the disposal of an asset, or an interest in an asset, by a member of a limited liability partnership has not accrued before the time of cessation of trade, the member shall be treated as if the chargeable gain accrued immediately before that time.

(3) In this section "the time of cessation of trade", in relation to a limited liability partnership, means the time when section 59A(1) ceases to apply in relation to the limited liability partnership."

11 Inheritance tax

In the Inheritance Tax Act 1984, after section 267 insert—

"267A Limited liability partnerships

For the purposes of this Act and any other enactments relating to inheritance tax—

(a) property to which a limited liability partnership is entitled, or which it occupies or uses, shall be treated as property to which its members are entitled, or which they occupy or use, as partners,

(b) any business carried on by a limited liability partnership shall be treated as carried on in partnership by its members,

(c) incorporation, change in membership or dissolution of a limited liability partnership shall be treated as formation, alteration or dissolution of a partnership, and

(d) any transfer of value made by or to a limited liability partnership shall be treated as made by or to its members in partnership (and not by or to the limited liability partnership as such)."

12 Stamp duty

(1) Stamp duty shall not be chargeable on an instrument by which property is conveyed or transferred by a person to a limited liability partnership in connection with its incorporation within the period of one year beginning with the date of incorporation if the following two conditions are satisfied.

(2) The first condition is that at the relevant time the person—

(a) is a partner in a partnership comprised of all the persons who are or are to be members of the limited liability partnership (and no-one else), or

(b) holds the property conveyed or transferred as nominee or bare trustee for one or more of the partners in such a partnership.

(3) The second condition is that—

(a) the proportions of the property conveyed or transferred to which the persons mentioned in subsection (2)(a) are entitled immediately after the conveyance or transfer are the same as those to which they were entitled at the relevant time, or

(b) none of the differences in those proportions has arisen as part of a scheme or arrangement of which the main purpose, or one of the main purposes, is avoidance of liability to any duty or tax.

(4) For the purposes of subsection (2) a person holds property as bare trustee for a partner if the partner has the exclusive right (subject only to satisfying any outstanding charge, lien or other right of the trustee to resort to the property for payment of duty, taxes, costs or other outgoings) to direct how the property shall be dealt with.

(5) In this section "the relevant time" means—

(a) if the person who conveyed or transferred the property to the limited liability partnership acquired the property after its incorporation, immediately after he acquired the property, and

(b) in any other case, immediately before its incorporation.

(6) An instrument in respect of which stamp duty is not chargeable by virtue of subsection (1) shall not be taken to be duly stamped unless—

(a) it has, in accordance with section 12 of the Stamp Act 1891, been stamped with a particular stamp denoting that it is not chargeable with any duty or that it is duly stamped, or

(b) it is stamped with the duty to which it would be liable apart from that subsection.

13 Class 4 national insurance contributions

In section 15 of the Social Security Contributions and Benefits Act 1992 and section 15 of the Social Security Contributions and Benefits (Northern Ireland) Act 1992 (Class 4 contributions), after subsection (3) insert—

"(3A) Where income tax is (or would be) charged on a member of a limited liability partnership in respect of profits or gains arising from the carrying on of a trade or profession by the limited liability partnership, Class 4 contributions shall be payable by him if they would be payable were the trade or profession carried on in partnership by the members."

Regulations

14 Insolvency and winding up

(1) Regulations shall make provision about the insolvency and winding up of limited liability partnerships by applying or incorporating, with such modifications as appear appropriate, Parts I to IV, VI and VII of the Insolvency Act 1986.

(2) Regulations may make other provision about the insolvency and winding up of limited liability partnerships, and provision about the insolvency and winding up of oversea limited liability partnerships, by—

(a) applying or incorporating, with such modifications as appear appropriate, any law relating to the insolvency or winding up of companies or other corporations which would not otherwise have effect in relation to them, or

(b) providing for any law relating to the insolvency or winding up of companies or other corporations which would otherwise have effect in relation to them not to apply to them or to apply to them with such modifications as appear appropriate.

(3) In this Act "oversea limited liability partnership" means a body incorporated or otherwise established outside Great Britain and having such connection with Great Britain, and such other features, as regulations may prescribe.

15   Application of company law etc

Regulations may make provision about limited liability partnerships and oversea limited liability partnerships (not being provision about insolvency or winding up) by—

(a)   applying or incorporating, with such modifications as appear appropriate, any law relating to companies or other corporations which would not otherwise have effect in relation to them,

(b)   providing for any law relating to companies or other corporations which would otherwise have effect in relation to them not to apply to them or to apply to them with such modifications as appear appropriate, or

(c)   applying or incorporating, with such modifications as appear appropriate, any law relating to partnerships.

16   Consequential amendments

(1)   Regulations may make in any enactment such amendments or repeals as appear appropriate in consequence of this Act or regulations made under it.

(2)   The regulations may, in particular, make amendments and repeals affecting companies or other corporations or partnerships.

17   General

(1)   In this Act "regulations" means regulations made by the Secretary of State by statutory instrument.

(2)   Regulations under this Act may in particular—

(a)   make provisions for dealing with non-compliance with any of the regulations (including the creation of criminal offences),

(b)   impose fees (which shall be paid into the Consolidated Fund), and

(c)   provide for the exercise of functions by persons prescribed by the regulations.

(3)   Regulations under this Act may—

(a)   contain any appropriate consequential, incidental, supplementary or transitional provisions or savings, and

(b)   make different provision for different purposes.

(4)   No regulations to which this subsection applies shall be made unless a draft of the statutory instrument containing the regulations (whether or

not together with other provisions) has been laid before, and approved by a resolution of, each House of Parliament.

(5) Subsection (4) applies to—

(a) regulations under section 14(2) not consisting entirely of the application or incorporation (with or without modifications) of provisions contained in or made under the Insolvency Act 1986,

(b) regulations under section 15 not consisting entirely of the application or incorporation (with or without modifications) of provisions contained in or made under Part I, Chapter VIII of Part V, Part VII, Parts XI to XIII, Parts XVI to XVIII, Part XX or Parts XXIV to XXVI of the Companies Act 1985,

(c) regulations under section 14 or 15 making provision about oversea limited liability partnerships, and

(d) regulations under section 16.

(6) A statutory instrument containing regulations under this Act shall (unless a draft of it has been approved by a resolution of each House of Parliament) be subject to annulment in pursuance of a resolution of either House of Parliament.

Supplementary

18 Interpretation

In this Act—

"address", in relation to a member of a limited liability partnership, means—

(a) if an individual, his usual residential address, and

(b) if a corporation or Scottish firm, its registered or principal office,

"business" includes every trade, profession and occupation,

"designated member" shall be construed in accordance with section 8,

"enactment" includes subordinate legislation (within the meaning of the Interpretation Act 1978),

"incorporation document" shall be construed in accordance with section 2,

"limited liability partnership" has the meaning given by section 1(2),

"member" shall be construed in accordance with section 4,

"modifications" includes additions and omissions,

"name", in relation to a member of a limited liability partnership, means—

(a) if an individual, his forename and surname (or, in the case of a peer or other person usually known by a title, his title instead of or in addition to either or both his forename and surname), and

(b) if a corporation or Scottish firm, its corporate or firm name,

"oversea limited liability partnership" has the meaning given by section 14(3),

"the registrar" means—

(a) if the registered office of the limited liability partnership is, or is to be, situated in England and Wales or in Wales, the registrar or other officer performing under the Companies Act 1985 the duty of registration of companies in England and Wales, and

(b) if its registered office is, or is to be, situated in Scotland, the registrar or other officer performing under that Act the duty of registration of companies in Scotland, and

"regulations" has the meaning given by section 17(1).

19 Commencement, extent and short title

(1) The preceding provisions of this Act shall come into force on such day as the Secretary of State may by order made by statutory instrument appoint; and different days may be appointed for different purposes.

(2) The Secretary of State may by order made by statutory instrument make any transitional provisions and savings which appear appropriate in connection with the coming into force of any provision of this Act.

(3) For the purposes of the Scotland Act 1998 this Act shall be taken to be a pre-commencement enactment within the meaning of that Act.

(4) Apart from sections 10 to 13 (and this section), this Act does not extend to Northern Ireland.

(5) This Act may be cited as the Limited Liability Partnerships Act 2000.

SCHEDULE
NAMES AND REGISTERED OFFICES

Section 1

Part I
Names

Index of names

1   In section 714(1) of the Companies Act 1985 (index of names), after
paragraph (d) insert—

"(da) limited liability partnerships incorporated under the Limited Liability
Partnerships Act 2000,".

Name to indicate status

2 (1) The name of a limited liability partnership must end with—

(a)   the expression "limited liability partnership", or

(b)   the abbreviation "llp" or "LLP".

(2)   But if the incorporation document for a limited liability partnership
states that the registered office is to be situated in Wales, its name must
end with—

(a)   one of the expressions "limited liability partnership" and "partneriaeth
atebolrwydd cyfyngedig", or

(b)   one of the abbreviations "llp", "LLP", "pac" and "PAC".

Registration of names

3 (1) A limited liability partnership shall not be registered by a name—

(a)   which includes, otherwise than at the end of the name, either of the
expressions "limited liability partnership" and "partneriaeth atebolrwydd
cyfyngedig" or any of the abbreviations "llp", "LLP", "pac" and "PAC",

(b)   which is the same as a name appearing in the index kept under section
714(1) of the Companies Act 1985,

(c)   the use of which by the limited liability partnership would in the opinion
of the Secretary of State constitute a criminal offence, or

(d) which in the opinion of the Secretary of State is offensive.

(2) Except with the approval of the Secretary of State, a limited liability partnership shall not be registered by a name which—

(a) in the opinion of the Secretary of State would be likely to give the impression that it is connected in any way with Her Majesty's Government or with any local authority, or

(b) includes any word or expression for the time being specified in regulations under section 29 of the Companies Act 1985 (names needing approval),

and in paragraph (a) "local authority" means any local authority within the meaning of the Local Government Act 1972 or the Local Government etc (Scotland) Act 1994, the Common Council of the City of London or the Council of the Isles of Scilly.

Change of name

4 (1) A limited liability partnership may change its name at any time.

(2) Where a limited liability partnership has been registered by a name which—

(a) is the same as or, in the opinion of the Secretary of State, too like a name appearing at the time of registration in the index kept under section 714(1) of the Companies Act 1985, or

(b) is the same as or, in the opinion of the Secretary of State, too like a name which should have appeared in the index at that time,

the Secretary of State may within twelve months of that time in writing direct the limited liability partnership to change its name within such period as he may specify.

(3) If it appears to the Secretary of State—

(a) that misleading information has been given for the purpose of the registration of a limited liability partnership by a particular name, or

(b) that undertakings or assurances have been given for that purpose and have not been fulfilled,

he may, within five years of the date of its registration by that name, in writing direct the limited liability partnership to change its name within such period as he may specify.

(4) If in the Secretary of State's opinion the name by which a limited liability partnership is registered gives so misleading an indication of the nature of its activities as to be likely to cause harm to the public, he may in writing direct the limited liability partnership to change its name within such period as he may specify.

(5) But the limited liability partnership may, within three weeks from the date of the direction apply to the court to set it aside and the court may set the direction aside or confirm it and, if it confirms it, shall specify the period within which it must be complied with.

(6) In sub-paragraph (5) "the court" means—

(a) if the registered office of the limited liability partnership is situated in England and Wales or in Wales, the High Court, and

(b) if it is situated in Scotland, the Court of Session.

(7) Where a direction has been given under sub-paragraph (2), (3) or (4) specifying a period within which a limited liability partnership is to change its name, the Secretary of State may at any time before that period ends extend it by a further direction in writing.

(8) If a limited liability partnership fails to comply with a direction under this paragraph—

(a) the limited liability partnership, and

(b) any designated member in default,

commits an offence.

(9) A person guilty of an offence under sub-paragraph (8) is liable on summary conviction to a fine not exceeding level 3 on the standard scale.

Notification of change of name

5 (1) Where a limited liability partnership changes its name it shall deliver notice of the change to the registrar.

(2) A notice delivered under sub-paragraph (1)—

(a) shall be in a form approved by the registrar, and

(b) shall be signed by a designated member of the limited liability partnership or authenticated in a manner approved by the registrar.

(3) Where the registrar receives a notice under sub-paragraph (2) he shall (unless the new name is one by which a limited liability partnership may not be registered)—

(a) enter the new name in the index kept under section 714(1) of the Companies Act 1985, and

(b) issue a certificate of the change of name.

(4) The change of name has effect from the date on which the certificate is issued.

Effect of change of name

6   A change of name by a limited liability partnership does not—

(a) affect any of its rights or duties,

(b) render defective any legal proceedings by or against it,

and any legal proceedings that might have been commenced or continued against it by its former name may be commenced or continued against it by its new name.

Improper use of "limited liability partnership" etc

7 (1) If any person carries on a business under a name or title which includes as the last words—

(a) the expression "limited liability partnership" or "partneriaeth atebolrwydd cyfyngedig", or

(b) any contraction or imitation of either of those expressions,

that person, unless a limited liability partnership or oversea limited liability partnership, commits an offence.

(2) A person guilty of an offence under sub-paragraph (1) is liable on summary conviction to a fine not exceeding level 3 on the standard scale.

Similarity of names

8   In determining for the purposes of this Part whether one name is the same as another there are to be disregarded—

(1) the definite article as the first word of the name,

(2) any of the following (or their Welsh equivalents or abbreviations of them or their Welsh equivalents) at the end of the name—

"limited liability partnership",

"company",

"and company",

"company limited",

"and company limited",

"limited",

"unlimited",

"public limited company",…

"investment company with variable capital", and

["open-ended investment company", and]

(3) type and case of letters, accents, spaces between letters and punctuation marks,

and "and" and "&" are to be taken as the same.

Part II
Registered Offices

Situation of registered office

9 (1) A limited liability partnership shall—

(a) at all times have a registered office situated in England and Wales or in Wales, or

(b) at all times have a registered office situated in Scotland,

to which communications and notices may be addressed.

(2) On the incorporation of a limited liability partnership the situation of its registered office shall be that stated in the incorporation document.

(3) Where the registered office of a limited liability partnership is situated in Wales, but the incorporation document does not state that it is to be situated in Wales (as opposed to England and Wales), the limited liability partnership may deliver notice to the registrar stating that its registered office is to be situated in Wales.

(4) A notice delivered under sub-paragraph (3)—

(a) shall be in a form approved by the registrar, and

(b) shall be signed by a designated member of the limited liability partnership or authenticated in a manner approved by the registrar.

Change of registered office

10 (1) A limited liability partnership may change its registered office by delivering notice of the change to the registrar.

(2) A notice delivered under sub-paragraph (1)—

(a) shall be in a form approved by the registrar, and

(b) shall be signed by a designated member of the limited liability partnership or authenticated in a manner approved by the registrar.

COMPANIES

Companies differ from partnerships in that they are bodies corporate. They have a separate personality from their members. The main advantage is limited liability.

Directors of companies have total control over the day-to-day operation of their companies. They act outside the control of the shareholders.

A company will continue to exist regardless of any changes in the membership. Shareholders may transfer their shares, or be bankrupted or die without affecting the day-to-day operation of a company's business.

Business debts of a company are owed by the company as a distinct legal person rather than the shareholders in the company.

Shareholders in a limited liability company are only liable for the amount remaining unpaid on their shareholding.

The incorporated company itself owns any business property.

If a registered company becomes insolvent and is wound up, a shareholder is only responsible for the company's debts up to the unpaid value on any shares held. If the shareholder holds fully paid shares, then he has no further liability to the company, or to its creditors, no matter the extent of the company's debt.

INTRODUCTION TO COMPANY LAW

A company is in law a corporation. It is an artificial legal "person". It has rights and obligations distinct from those of its members.

The Companies Act 1985 is the most important source of company law. The 1985 Act is a consolidating act which brings together legislation contained in a number of earlier companies acts The 1985 Act has been amended in significant respects by the Insolvency Act 1986 and the Companies (Amendment) Act 1989. The 1985 Act applies throughout Great Britain

LEGAL PERSONALITY

You all must have heard the term LEGAL PERSONALITY. The word personality derives from the Latin PER (through) and SONARE (to sound).
In law, a person does not need arms and legs. Obviously we are all persons in law, but so are entities like registered companies. An entity which is capable of separate legal identity—as the possessor of legal rights, responsible for the performance of legal duties—is a person as far as the law is concerned.
When we speak of natural persons we mean humans. When we speak of legal or juristic persons we mean separate entities like companies.

But partnerships, clubs and trade unions are NOT legal persons. They have no legal existence apart from the people of whom they are composed.

A legal person is created by the process of incorporation. It is a corporation, from the Latin CORPUS (a body). It has a separate legal identity apart from the human beings who work for it. People come and go but the corporation lives on, unless it is brought to an end by the proper legal processes. There are corporations sole and corporations aggregate.
Corporations sole are official positions like The Archbishop of Canterbury. There is a great deal of property vested in such positions. It may be used by the incumbents but it is not their personal property.
But corporations aggregate are the million companies registered in England and Wales. They are classified according to their method of creation.

CREATION OF CORPORATIONS

BY ROYAL CHARTER

This is issued after a request to the Privy Council, the Highest Court in the land. Examples of chartered corporations are the BBC, The Institute of Chartered Accountants, the Chartered Institute of Management. Liability of members is not usually limited, but usually there is no trading, so it is not important.

BY ACT OF PARLIAMENT

Statutory corporations are generally large bodies of a public nature. The 19th Century railway and canal companies were formed by statute but this does not happen anymore.

BY REGISTRATION

This is done under the Companies Acts and this is the way most trading corporations are established.

The limited company has come to dominate the organisation of business activity. The limited company form is very flexible. That is why it is used by businesses of widely different sizes and needs, from the one-person business to the transnational corporation with a host of subsidiary companies.

Limited companies differ from partnerships. Limited companies have a separate personality from their members. The main advantage of this separate personality is limited liability. Also in a limited company, it is the directors who have almost total control over the day-to-day operation of their companies and they act outside the control of the owners (shareholders). Also a limited company can have various types of share capital. It can have a debenture loan capital even.

The limited company has <u>perpetual succession</u> which means that the company will continue to exist regardless of any changes in the membership. Shareholders may transfer their shares, or be declared bankrupt or even die, without in any way affecting the day-to-day operation of the company's business.

Also, within the limited company form, any <u>business debts </u>are owed by the company as a distinct legal person rather than by the shareholders in the company. Shareholders in limited liability companies are only liable for the amount remaining unpaid on their shareholding. But any such debts owed by shareholders in a limited liability company are owed to the company as a distinct legal personality in the view of the law and NOT directly to the company's creditors. This means that creditors have no direct claim against shareholders even where those shareholders hold shares that remain unpaid. The effect of these provisions is that if shareholders in a company have paid up the full nominal value of their shares, then they are free from any further claim and cannot be forced to accept any further debt or commitment.

Because of the doctrine of separate legal personality, the incorporated company itself owns any <u>business property</u>. So shareholders have no proprietary interest in the concrete assets owned by the company. Their only interest is in the dividends declared, based on profitable performance of those assets. So when shares change hands, property deeds and titles are not affected.

Individual members of a limited company CAN enter into contracts with their companies.

A limited company can raise <u>capital</u>. A limited company is permitted to borrow capital via debentures or loan stock. Limited companies can secure debts by means of a "floating charge" which are not fixed on particular assets but are secured against the company's property in its stock-in-trade, which is changing constantly and being dealt with in the course of the company's business.

Shareholders of public limited companies are merely passive and indirectly engaged in the enterprises in which they have bought shares. The directors and managers of companies are therefore agents of companies.

The main advantage of a limited company form is the fact that it brings with it <u>limited liability</u>.

THE COMPANY'S OWN REGULATION

A great deal of freedom of choice is given to each individual company as to how it will be administered. To do so, each company has a set of regulations known as Articles of Association. These are usually specially prepared by the person who assists with the formation, but the Companies Act provides a model form of articles (TABLE A) and most of the regulations adopted by a company will follow that model. The provisions of Table A are contained in a statutory instrument (SI 1985 No.805) which came into force with the 1985 Act. Companies formed before the 1985 Act usually have regulations based on earlier versions of Table A.

THE GENERAL LAW

The general law applies to companies as it applies to individuals. The general law of contract, for example, applies to companies, as does the law of tort, conveyancing, etc.

REGISTRATION

Companies have to be registered at Companies House in Cardiff. When registered, the Registrar issues a certificate of incorporation.

Companies can be companies "limited by shares", one type of company.This means that the members (or shareholders) have a limited liability to pay the debts of the company. When new shares are issued by a company, the person who takes the shares must agree to pay for them. Usually payment will be made immediately but sometimes the shares will be issued "unpaid" or "partly paid", in which case payment must be made later. If the company goes into liquidation and is insolvent the members are liable to pay for their shares in full if they have not already done so. This really means that a member who has paid for his shares stands to lose his shares but nothing more on the insolvency of the company; a member who has not paid for his shares in full stands to lose his shares and the unpaid amount but nothing more.

The position of a shareholder in a limited company is quite different from the position of a member of a partnership. If a partnership business fails, each of the partners stands to lose not only what he has invested but also any private wealth which he may have.

COMPANIES LIMITED BY SHARES

A small number of companies are limited by guarantee rather than by shares. This means that each member undertakes to pay a specified amount if the company is wound up while he is a member or within a year after he ceases to be a member. The main difference between this type of company and a company limited by shares is that the guarantee does not become payable until the company is wound up, whereas shares must be paid for immediately or when the company requires payment.

Most companies limited by guarantee are charities or other non-trading companies. One advantage of being limited by guarantee is that the company can apply for dispensation to drop the word "limited" from the name of the company. (s 30 CA 1985) whereas a company limited by shares cannot.

UNLIMITED COMPANIES

An unlimited company is one which is registered under the Companies Act but without any limit on the liability of the members. If an unlimited company goes into liquidation the m3embers are liable to contribute the whole of their private wealth to the payment of the company's debts. The creditors cannot sue the members direct but must claim in the liquidation. The liquidator then calls for contributions from the members. The main advantage of an unlimited company is that it is exempt from the requirement of publishing its accounts.

PUBLIC COMPANY

A plc public company has to have a certificate issued by the Registrar of Companies showing the authorised minimum share capital, currently £50,000. It must have at least 2 directors. It can issue debentures. It must submit its accounts within 7 months of the end of its accounting period. Its directors must retire when they reach 70 years of age.

All companies are either public or private but there are other types within these categories:

QUOTED COMPANY

A company is in this category if its shares are quoted on a stock exchange. A quoted company must keep a special register of those shareholders with 5% or more of their shares. Only public companies are quoted companies (Stock Exchange Rules).

CLOSE COMPANIES

This category is relevant only for tax purposes, because special tax rules apply to close companies. All private companies are close companies and some public companies are too.

SMALL AND MEDIUM SIZED COMPANIES

These are companies which because of their relatively small size (in financial terms) are exempt from providing certain information in their accounts.

PARTNERSHIP COMPANY

This category will in most respects be an ordinary private company but with regulations suitable for a company which is owned by its own employees.

COMPANY FORMATION

The solicitor who is asked to form a company on behalf of a trader must first discuss with him whether a company is, in fact, the appropriate medium through which to operate.

The solicitor must :

1. Discuss with the client the effect of incorporation and the legal requirements of running a company.
2. Discuss with the client whether the company should be formed by the solicitor or whether an existing company should be bought off the peg from a firm of law stationers.
3. Prepare the documents leading to incorporation.
4. Inform the client as to the steps to be taken after incorporation, as required by the Companies Act 1985.
5. Advise the client as to the problems which may arise if contracts are made in the name of, or on behalf of, the company before incorporation.

STEPS LEADING TO INCORPORATION

For a company to be registered under the Companies Act, the promoters (the traders who wish to form a company) ot their agents (a solicitor or a law stationer) must deliver to the Registrar of Companies the following:

1. a memorandum of association;
2. articles of association;

3. Form G10, setting out details of the egistered office, the directors and secretary of the company;

4. Form G12—a statutory declaration of compliance with the requirements of theCompanies Act;

5. the Registrar's fee.

MEMORANDUM OF ASSOCIATION

Section 1 CA 1985 provides that every company must have a memorandum, which is sometimes described as the company's "charter". Its principle function is to set out the reason for the company and to regulate its dealings with outsiders. The Companies Regulations 1985 (Tables A top F) set out model memoranda. Table B is applicable to a private company limited by shares. Five compulsory clauses MUST be included in the memorandum. These relate to:

1. the name of the company;

2. the registered office;

3. the liability of the members;

4. the authorised capital of the company.

The memorandum must contain the "association" clause and the "subscription" clause.

The "association" clause states that the persons who subscribe (sign) the memorandum wish to be formed into a company and that they agree to a specified number of shares in the new company.

The "subscription" clause sets out the names, addresses and descriptions of the subscribers and the number of shares each agrees to take.

The memorandum must be signed by a minimum of two subscribers, who sign in the presence of one witness. Each subscriber must agree to take at least one share.

THE NAME OF THE COMPANY

Generally there is freedom of choice as far as the company's name is concerned. The purpose of a company's name is to differentiate the company from other registered companies. Section 25 and 26 CA 1985 prohibits the Registrar from registering a company with a name which:-

1. Does NOT end with the word LTD if the company is a private limited company. But section 30 allows a company limited by guarantee to forego this rule as long as the guarantee company does not pay dividends.

If the name is rejected by the Registrar, the promoter will have to submit a further set of documents applying for formation with a new name. The new memorandum will have to be printed and new articles. Section 28 CA 1985 states that, after a company is formed, it is free to change its name by passing a special resolution subject to the same restrictions as apply to choice of name by a new company. Section 28 also gives the Registrar the power to DIRECT a change of name within 12c months of registration if it is the same as or too similar to a name which is or should be on the index. The Registrar hasw the power to direct a company to change its registered name if it gives so misleading an indication of the nature of its activities as to be likely to cause harm to the public (section 32 CA 1985).

THE REGISTERED OFFICE

The second compulsory clause in the memorandum sets out the situation of the company's registered office. It does nhot state the address of the company office (this appears on Form G10) bu8t only that the office is in England or Wales. This is so as to determine the company's domicile.

THE OBJECTS AND ULTRA VIRES DOCTRINE

The third compulsory clause in the memorandumis its objects. Any contracts made, or acts done, by the company not within the objects clause or reasonably incidental thereto, may be void. This clause should have drafted into it such items:

a) a power to borrow

b) a power to buy land

c) a power to take over or merge with other businesses or set up subsidiaries

d) a power to invest the company's money

e) a power to sell the business

f) a power to lend or guarantee loans.

THE LIABILITY CLAUSE

This clause states whether the members' liability is limited. The clause is unalterable.

THE CAPITAL CLAUSE
This clause in the memorandum states the amount of the company's authorised share capital and how it is divided into shares of a specified nominal value.

THE ARTICLES OF ASSOCIATION

The second document which must be considered before a company is incorporated is the articles of association Section 7 CA 1985). These regulate the company's internal affairs and contain the regulations dealing with such matters as directors' powers, proceedings at members' meetings and so on. The promoters decide which form the articles take.

There are no compulsory clauses but the Companies Regulations (Tables a to F) contain a standard set of articles which contain regulations (Table A) intended to be suitable for an average company. Other than Table A additional articles which can be included are those which deal with :-

a) giving authority under section 80 CA 1985 to directors to issue shares

b) the exclusion, extension or variation of rights under section 89ff CA 1985

c) the removal of directors

d) additional voting power to a director so that he can only be removed with his consent

e) a power to remove a director which dispenses ith the necessity of a special notice under section 379 CA 1985.

FORM G10

This is a statutory form required by section 10(2) and Schedule 1 CA 1985 which is a statement of the first directors and secretary and intended situation of the company's registered office. The form is supplied with guidance notes for completion.

The address of the company's first registered office appears in this form, not in the memorandum; later it can be moved anywhere within the country provided the Registrar is notified within 14 days of the change. A prescribed form (Form G287) is used for this purpose.

b) The company must have at least one director and if only one is appointed he must also NOT be the company secretary. This ensures that every company has at least two separate officers.

c) The information required in relation to the directors includes details of other directorships.

d) The persons names as directors and secretary, and who sign the form to signify their consent, automatically become the first directors and secretary of the company even if the articles provide otherwise.

FORM G12
This is the statutory declaration of compliance with the registration requirements of the Act. It must be completed by the solicitor engaged in forming the company or one of the company's directors or secretary named in Form G10.

THE FEE
The documents must be sent with the correct fee to the Registrar of Companies.

THE CERTIFICATE OF INCORPORATION

The Registrar will examine the documents and, provided they are in order,and the chosen name is still available. He will sign a certificate of incorporation stating that the company was incorporated under the Companies Act 1985 and that the company is limited He will specify the company's registered number on the certificate. This number must be used on all official documents and business letters.The company becomes a legal entity from the date of the certificate of incorporation. The Registrar will p-lace a notice to this effect in the Government's Official newspaper.

Once the company is registered it must keep certain records at its registered office:

1. A register and index of members, containing each member's name, address, date of entry on the register and cessation of membership and details of shares held.

    1. A register of directors and a register of secretaries setting out their names, addresses, and for directors only, details of any other directorships. It is advisable to include details of the period of holding office since problems may arise in the future as to whether a board decision

was validly passed and enquiries of the directors holding office at the time may be necessary; similarly for secretaries.

2. A register of the interests of directors, their spouses and infant children in shares and debentures of the company, its holdings and subsidiary companies as required by sections 324 to 328 CA 1985. The purpose of this is toensure that the extent of a director's direct or indirect control over the company is known.

3. A register of charges which must be kept ven if the company has not yet charged any of its assets. It sets out details of the property charged and the terms of the charge.

4. Copies of the companies memorandum and articles.

All these books must be available for inspection by members, creditors and the general public for at least 2 hours daily during business hours.

The directors' service contracts must be kept here also and can only be inspected by members.

The minute book of general meetings of the company can be inspected only by members but should be kept here also.

Rights and duties

Directors' Duties

Directors owe a variety of duties to their companies. Directors are under a general duty to act bona fide in the interests of the company. For example, they must not use the powers they have been given for an improper or collateral purpose. (Howard Smith v Ampol Petroleum [1974]).

Directors have a duty not to permit a conflict of interest and duty to arise. Directors must not obtain a personal profit from their position within the company. (Regal (Hastings) v Gulliver [1942]).

Criminalisation of employers' conduct

Statute has intervened to criminalize the conduct of those who use their position as directors to benefit themselves through the insider dealing legislation, for example. Sections 52 and 57(2) of the Criminal Justice Act 1993 refers to and prohibits directors from dealing in shares on the basis of inside information they gained from their positions.

Directors must show the duty of skill and care. (Lagunas Nitrate Co v Lagunas Syndicate [1989]).

In the absence of any grounds of suspicion, directors are entitled to leave the day to day operation of the company's business in the hands of managers and to trust them to perform their tasks honestly.

CASE LAW

Salomon v A Salomon & Co Ltd [1897] AC 33, HL
Boot manufacturer as sole trader for over 30 years.
Company was formed to purchase the business
Mr Salomon 94 of the shares and six members of his family owned one share each as nominees him
The purchase price £39,000 paid by:

- £10,000 worth of fully paid shares;

- debenture worth £10,000 secured over the company; and

- the balance by the company discharging of Mr S's trade debts and liabilities

In less than one year the company had trading difficulties and went into liquidation. Mr S brought proceedings to enforce the debenture. If successful he would be paid first. There were not enough assets to discharge the debenture so the other creditors would get nothing. The liquidator objected saying that the debenture was invalid as a 'fraud', ie forming a one man company amounted to a fraud. Both the court of first instance and the CA found that the company as nothing more than Mr S's nominee, refused to recognise its existence as a separate legal person and decided in favour of the liquidator.
Held The company exists at law as a separate being from its shareholders and it made no difference that one member owned the beneficially all or substantially all of the shares. Mr S's debenture was valid.

Macaura v Northern Assurance Co [1925] AC 619, HL
Mr Macaura owned timber estates in Ireland and sold the timber to a company for £42,000 paid by the issue of 42,000 fully paid shares. He had also financed the company for about £19,000 as an unsecured creditor. He took out insurance on the timber in his name, but when most of the timber was destroyed by fire, the insurance company refused to pay.

Held The claim failed. The timber was owned by the company and not by him so he had no insurable interest in it. It made no difference that Mr M the only shareholder and a major creditor, because the company was an independent entity.

Parke v The Daily News Ltd [1962] 2 All ER 929

The defendant company published and printed two newspapers and carried on certain subsidiary activities. In view of losses incurred by the two newspapers the defendants sold them to another company, but continued in business with their subsidiary activities. The defendants proposed to pay the balance of the purchase price received for the newspapers, after meeting costs of the transaction, as compensation to those of their employees who had lost their jobs when the newspaper ceased publication. The plaintiff, a shareholder, was granted an injunction restraining the payment, which was undertaken, not in the interests of the shareholders, but as a gift of a large part of the company's funds, with the object of treating the employees generously and beyond all entitlement. Such a payment was *ultra vires* and therefore void.

Lee v Lee's Air Farming ltd [1961] AC 12, PC

The appellant was the widow of
Mr Lee owned 2,999 of the 3,000 shares in the company, which carried on an aerial crop spraying business. He was its sole director, had been employed by it and was killed in an air crash while working. His widow claimed compensation under the New Zealand Workers Compensation Act 1922 and the question arose as to whether he was a 'worker' within the meaning of that legislation. The New Zealand CA had found that for all intents and purposes he was the company and as such was the employer so could not be a worker.
Held The appeal was allowed applying Salomon v Salomon. The company had a separate legal personality so contractual relations could exist between him and it.

DHN Food Distributors Ltd v Tower Hamlets London Borough Council [1976] 1 WLR 852, CA

DHN Food Distributors Ltd carried on a food distribution business and had two wholly-owned subsidiaries, all with the same directors. The subsidiaries were Bronze Investments Ltd, which owned the land used in the business, and DHN Food Transport Ltd, which owned the lorries. The local authority issued a compulsory purchase order over the land and paid compensation for the land value to Bronze Investments Ltd, but it refused to pay compensation disturbance to the business. The business was carried on by the parent company and not Bronze and the parent was a separate legal entity and not subject to the CPO

Held Lord Denning lifted the corporate veil on the basis that, on the facts of the case the doctrine of corporate personality was applied artificially and unfairly. He treated the group as one entity for the purposes of that particular statute. DHN Food Distributors Ltd should receive compensation for business disruption to its business.

Whaley Bridge Calico Printing Co v Green [1880] 5 QBD 109

Bowen J said:

'The term promoter is a term not of law, but of business, usefully summing up in a single word a number of business operations familiar to the commercial world by which a company is generally brought into existence.'

What the promoter does as analogous to a trustee for the company's benefit. So a company may enforce the personal claims of a promoter against a party who has undertaken to pay the promoter a profit or other benefit in connection with its promotion.

Gluckstein v Barnes [1900] AC 240, HL

The National Agricultural Hall Co Ltd went into liquidation and Mr Gluckstein and three other purchased its premises for £140,000 and re-sold them for £180,000 to a Olympia Company Ltd, a company they had promoted. In the prospectus they disclosed the £40,000 profit, but they did not disclose the £20,000 profit they made out of dome discounted debentures of the old company. The new company, Olympia, went into liquidation and the liquidator claimed Mr G's share of the £20,000.

Held (Upholding the findings of the lower courts)' Mr G was liable to account to the company for the amount sought. The directors of the company were Mr G and his associates and were not independent. It was therefore not sufficient that knew the details, but full disclosure should have been made to the company.

Phonogram Ltd v Lane [1982] QB 938, CA

It was planned to form a new company to manage, 'Cheap Mean & Nasty' was the name of a rock band, which was to be managed by a new company to be called Fragile Management Ltd. Before Fragile was formed Mr Lane, who was promoting it, entered negotiations with Phonogram Ltd and for a loan 'for and on behalf of' the proposed company. The load was made but the company was

never formed and an action was brought against Mr Lane for repayment of the money.
Held Mr L was personally liable to repay the loan.

Rayfield v Hands [1958] 2 All ER 194

The articles of association of a private company provided:

> 'Every member who intends to transfer his shares shall inform the directors who will take the said shares equally between them at a fair value.'

The plaintiff wished to sell his shares and asked the three directors of the company to buy them in accordance with the articles, but they refused. He sued them without joining the company in the action.
Held The court found that the directors were bound to buy the shares. The articles were to create a contractual relationship between the plaintiff as shareholder and vendor and the defendants as directors and purchasers. Vaisey J dealt with the problems raised by the reasoning of the courts examined below, 4.1.3 by saying:

> Now the question arises at the outset whether the terms of [the] article...relate to the rights of the members *inter se*...or whether the relationship is between a member as such and directors as such, I may dispose of this point very briefly by saying that, in my judgment, the relationship here is between the plaintiff as a member and the defendants not as directors but as members.

The said that this might not apply to all companies but this was a quasi-partnership in which the directors owned all of the shares between them.

Ashbury Railway Carriage & Iron Co Ltd v Riche [1875] LR 7 HL 653

The company bought a concession to build a railway in Belgium and entered into an agreement with Mr Riche to finance its construction. The company got into difficulties the contract with Mr R was repudiated and Mr R sued for damages. The company in its defence argued that the financing agreement was void and ineffective as it was *ultra vires* its powers. The objects clause in its memorandum of association empowered the company to make railway carriages and rolling stock, to carry on business as mechanical engineers, and to trade in timber, coal, metals etc.
Held The agreement was *ultra vires* and therefore void. Lord Cairns LC emphasised that the memorandum states the outer limits of what constitutes a company's 'vitality and power'. It cannot exceed those limits. Even if all the

shareholders unanimously consent, it makes no difference; if a contract is beyond the competence and power of a company, then it is void *ab initio* and nothing the members subsequently do can save it.

Cotman v Brougham [1918] AC 514, HL

The objects clause of a company included power to carry on almost every type of commercial activity and had a final sub-clause stating that each sub-clause should be construed as a separate and independent object. A dispute arose as to whether or not the company was authorised to underwrite a share issue in another company.

Held The objects clause of the memorandum was so widely drafted that the transaction was in fact *intra vires*.

Bell Houses Ltd v City Wall Properties Ltd [1966] 2 All ER 674, CA

The plaintiff company's business was as a property developer in accordance with its objects clause. It put the defendant company in touch with a financier but the introducer's fee was not paid on the grounds that mortgage broking was *ultra vires* its plaintiff's business, so it was not entitled to the fee. The plaintiff's objects clause contained a phrase permitting it 'to carry on any other trade or business whatsoever which can, in the opinion of the board of directors, be advantageously carried on by the company in connection with or as ancillary to any of the above businesses or the general business of the company'.

Held The plain and natural meaning of the sub-clause was such as to render this ancillary business *intra vires*.

Re Introductions Ltd (1970) CA

This company started business offering hospitality services, then changed to deck chair rental and finally pig breeding, after which it went into liquidation. When the bank tried to enforce its security but the liquidator that it was unenforceable as the company's borrowing had been *ultra vires* and so the security granted was void. The company's memorandum contained a wide objects clause in similar terms to that used in *Cotman v Brougham*. It did not include pig farming but one sub-clauses gave power to borrow. The bank knew of the purpose of the loan.

Held The breeding of pigs was clearly *ultra vires* and the bank had notice of it. Borrowing is not capable of being an independent substantive object and is no more than an incidental power. It cannot be elevated to an object by the wording of the memorandum. Borrowing for the purposes of an *ultra vires* object (pig breeding) was not an *intra vires* object.

Southern Foundries (1926) Ltd v Shirlaw [1940] AC, HL

Mr Shirlaw had been appointed managing director of Southern Foundries Ltd in 1933 pursuant to a written agreement. Southern Foundries Ltd was taken over by Federated Industries Ltd in 1936 and altered its articles of association to insert a new article which empowered Federated Industries Ltd, by written instrument, to remove any of its directors. In 1937, Federated Industries Ltd used that power to remove Mr S from office and the latter sued for breach of contract.

Held Mr S was awarded damages. Lord Porter stated as a matter of general principle:

A company cannot be precluded from altering its articles thereby giving itself power to act upon the provisions of its altered articles—but so to act may nevertheless be a breach of contract if it is contrary to a stipulation validly made before the alteration. Nor can an injunction be granted to prevent the adoption of the new articles and in that sense they are binding on all and sundry, but for the company to act upon them will none the less render it liable in damages if such action is contrary to the previous engagements of the company.

Morgan v Grey [1953] Ch 83

As long as his name remains on the register of members, a shareholder who becomes bankrupt (although he must vote in accordance with the instructions of his trustee in bankruptcy), even if the articles provide that notices of meetings are to be sent to the trustee in bankruptcy.

Exxon Corp v Exxon Insurance Consultants International Ltd [1982] 1 Ch 119

Exxon Corp an global oil company sought an injunction preventing Exxon Insurance was a motor insurance brokers from using of the word 'Exxon' in its company name.

Held The common law tort of passing off extended to prevent the Exxon Insurance from using the name 'Exxon' even though it was not in the same business as the plaintiff. Because the name 'Exxon' is so widely known, it was possible that the sue of that name might lead the public to do business with the defendant company under the impression that a connection exists the companies.

White v Bristol Aeroplane Ltd (1953) CA

The company had preference shares and ordinary shares. A bonus issue was proposed of both preference and ordinary shares which would have the effect of proportionately increasing the number of ordinary shares in issue in relation to the preference shares in issue. The literal voting rights of both classes were unaffected by the bonus issue but the ordinary shareholders' relative voting strength was increased afterwards simply because there were more of them. The preference shareholders challenged the bonus issue arguing that it constituted a variation of their class rights and they should have the protection of the s 125 procedure.

Held The Court of Appeal rejected the preference shareholders' argument.

Cumbrian Newspapers Group Ltd v Cumberland and Westmorland Herald Newspaper and Printing Co Ltd (1986)

The plaintiff company had, as part of a scheme of amalgamation, acquired 10.67% of the ordinary shares of the defendant company. In order to make it difficult for anyone outside the Cumbrian Newspapers Group Ltd to ever gain control of newspapers owned by the defendant company, the articles of association of the defendant company were altered so that the plaintiff company had three types of special right attaching to any ordinary shares it held in the defendant at any time. These three categories of rights were: (1) rights of preemption on the transfer of any other issued ordinary shares in the defendant company; (2) pre-emption rights over any unissued shares in the defendant company; (3) the right to appoint a director of the defendant so long as the plaintiff owned at least 10% of its shares. The question before the court was— if the company wanted to alter those particular articles, did this constitute a variation of class rights even though the 'class' was defined by reference to any ordinary shares held by one person?

Held These rights, although they did not attach to particular shares but inured to an individual, were still capable of being 'class rights'.

Re BML Group Ltd [1994] 2 BCLC 674, CA

A shareholders' agreement was in existence and it provided that a meeting of the company was only quorate if B or his proxy were present at it. A resolution to remove B as a director was passed at a meeting in his absence and he brought a s459 action in protest at his removal.

Held The Court of Appeal upheld the effect of the shareholders' agreement saying that B's rights were in effect class rights which could not be overridden. They had the same effect as if they were class rights contained in the company's articles of association.

Re Halt Garage (1964) Ltd (1982)

Mr and Mrs C were the sole directors of the company and owned all its shares. They both worked in the business, drawing directors' remuneration as authorised to do under the company's constitution. However, Mrs C became ill in 1967 and withdrew from involvement in the company's business. She continued to be a director and received payment as such at a reduced rate. By 1968, the company was no longer profitable and it went into insolvent liquidation in 1971. The liquidator applied for repayment of sums allegedly overpaid to Mr and Mrs C as directors' remuneration. He argued that Mrs C should not have been entitled to any remuneration from the time she became ill onwards and that the level of Mr C's remuneration was unreasonable and disproportionate to the benefit gained by the company in the light of the company's unprofitability.

Held The liquidator's claim against Mr C failed as the court thought that it was not for the courts to pronounce on the level of directors' remuneration but rather this was a question for the shareholders and in the absence of fraud or of the company making a distribution of its capital then although the law required shareholders to be honest it did not require them to be wise in setting the level of directors' remuneration.

However, the court agreed with the liquidator with regard to those sums paid to Mrs C, ostensibly as remuneration, after she had become ill and withdrawn from active participation in the company. This, said the court, was not genuine remuneration but was a disguised gift of capital and thus repayable to the company

John v Rees (1969)

The plaintiff was the president and chairman of the Pembrokeshire Divisional Labour Party. At a properly constituted meeting, a conflict of views arose and there was evidence of noise, disorder and some minor violence. The plaintiff, as chairman, warned that it would be impossible to continue the meeting if the disorder persisted. Upon the continuance of the disorder, the chairman announced the adjournment of the meeting and left, accompanied by a number of others. The meeting continued without the chairman and new officers were elected. The plaintiff sought an order invalidating these actions.

Held The chairman possessed an inherent power to adjourn a meeting in the event of disorder if he acted *bona fide* and if the adjournment were for no longer than necessary for the restoration of order. However, in the present case, the disorder was not sufficient to warrant an adjournment. The meeting remained in being and the elections of the new officers were thus valid.

R v Bradley [1961] 1 All ER 669

The period of disqualification of a director runs from the date of conviction. The Court cannot order it to run from the date of release, even if the sentence of imprisonment exceeds 5 years.

Re Transplanters (Holdings) Ltd [1958] 2 All ER 711

Where a director to whom the company owes a debt which is statute-barred subsequently signs a balance sheet on which the debt is shown, he is acting in breach of his fiduciary duty as he is personally interested in the debt, and the balance sheet cannot constitute an acknowledgement to revive the debt under the Limitation Act 1939.

Re Bolton Engineering Co Ltd [1956] 1 All ER 799

A trustee in bankruptcy who has not obtained registration of the bankrupt's shares in his own name is not a 'contributory' for the purpose of presenting a petition: his powers to represent the bankrupt under section 216 do not take effect after a winding-up order has been made.

Re Duomatic Ltd (1969)

For a period of 15 months, the two directors of the company were its only ordinary shareholders. Under the articles of the company, remuneration of directors had to be determined from time to time by resolution of the company in general meeting. No such resolutions were passed but the two directors drew sums according to their needs and entered them into the accounts as 'directors' salaries'. The liquidator of the company sought to recover these sums from the two directors.

Held Although none of the payments were authorised by resolution, the clear assent of all the ordinary shareholders was as binding as a resolution and the payments could not be disturbed. Buckley J said: 'Where it can be shown that all the shareholders who have a right to attend and vote at a general meeting of the company assent to some matter which a general meeting of the company could carry into effect, that assent is as binding as a resolution in general meeting would be.'

Cane v Jones (1980)

Two brothers, H and P, formed a company and were the sole directors of that company. The shareholding of the company was divided equally between members of H's family and members of P's family. The company's articles provided for the election of a chairman by the directors, who should have a casting vote at board meetings and should preside over and have a casting vote at general meetings of the company. An agreement was made between all the shareholders that the chairman should cease to be entitled to use his casting vote. The management of the company became deadlocked. The plaintiff claimed the informal agreement was effective to alter the company's articles, and thus the defendants could not exercise a casting vote.

Held Despite the lack of a meeting or a resolution in writing to comply with the statutory requirements regarding the alteration of a company's articles, the agreement was effective. The agreement represented the unanimous will of the shareholders acting together and had the same effect as would a special resolution altering the company's articles so as to deprive the chairman of his casting vote.

Quin & Axtens Ltd v Salmon (1909) HL

The articles of association of the appellant company vested in the directors the general management of the company. With regard to certain matters, however, the articles provided that no resolution of the directors should be valid if either of the two managing directors dissented. The respondent, one of the two managing directors, so dissented from such a resolution. At an extraordinary general meeting, the company purported to ratify the original resolution by a simple majority. The respondent, as original plaintiff, was granted an injunction restraining the company from acting on the resolutions of the board and the general meeting. The company appealed.

Held The House of Lords dismissed the appeal. The resolutions were inconsistent with the provisions of the articles and the company was properly restrained from acting thereon. The right of management veto, as contained in the articles, was therefore upheld.

Bushell v Faith [1970] AC, HL

The Company had 300 shares issued. The plaintiff, defendant and their sister held 100 each. The plaintiff and the defendant were the only directors. The company's articles of association weighted the voting rights attached to the shares from the normal one vote per share to three votes per share where, and only where, the issue before a general meeting of the company was the removal of the director holding those shares. The plaintiff and her sister tried to remove the defendant from office as a director. The issue thus arose as to whether a court should give effect to the weighted voting rights attached by the articles to the defendant's shares which would, if recognised, have the effect of blocking the resolution to remove him by 300 votes to 200.

Held The House of Lords decided to recognise the weighted voting rights accorded by the articles. In so doing they drew a distinction between the voting rights attached to shares and the mandatory scope of s303 of the Companies Act 1985. They thought that Parliament, in enacting s303, did not mean to fetter the scope for a company to issue a share with such rights or restrictions attaching to the share as the company saw fit.

Wright v Atlas Wright (Europe) Ltd (1999) CA

The plaintiffs sold the entire share capital of a company to the defendant company and agreed that, on their retirement, the defendant company would make annual payments to them 'for life'. The company duly paid the agreed sums for seven years. After that time, the shareholding in the defendant company was again sold. The new directors declined to continue the payments and, when sued by the plaintiffs, the company argued that the agreement for such payments was contrary to s 319 since it could not be terminated by the company and it had not been formally approved by the company in general meeting.

Held The Court of Appeal upheld the first instance judgment and determined that s 319 was one of the provisions on company law which was subject to the principle in *Re Duomatic Ltd* (1969) in that, provided all the then shareholders were apprised of and agreed to the contract, such consent would override the requirement for' the passing of a formal resolution at a meeting.

Craven Ellis v Canons Ltd [1936] 2 KB, CA

The plaintiff had been purportedly appointed managing director of the defendant company by an agreement which set out a rate of remuneration payable but was in actual fact void as the directors of the company were not qualified to act as such under the articles. The company now relied on this want of authority in the plaintiff's appointment in its refusal to pay him for the services of managing director which he had already rendered to the company.

Held Despite the fact that his appointment as managing director was void the plaintiff was still entitled to payment on a *quantum meruit* basis.

Guinness plc v Saunders [1990] 1 All ER 652, HL

In 1986 Guinness plc launched a contested takeover bid for the Distillers brewing group. During the course of its bid Guinness formed an executive committee of its directors Mr Roux, Mr Saunders and Mr Ward known as 'the war cabinet'. Mr Ward was a US lawyer and all three were members of the board of directors of Guinness plc. A Jersey-based company owned by Mr Ward provided consultancy advice to Guinness during the bid and was paid a fee of £5.2 million. This fee had, allegedly, been agreed by the war cabinet, but not by the main board of Guinness. Indeed, the main board of directors was not appraised of this payment at all. Guinness sought repayment of this fee on the grounds that the failure to disclose to the board the payment to one of the directors was a breach of fiduciary duty on the part of Mr Ward. He in turn tried to argue that it was remuneration which he was entitled to under Guinness plc's articles of association.

Held The House of Lords held that the contract to pay Mr Ward was void and he was not entitled to keep this sum. Guinness' articles of association did not empower the 'war cabinet' to approve this payment as special remuneration. Neither could Mr Ward rely on another of Guinness' articles which entitled a director acting in another professional capacity to be remunerated as such for work undertaken in that capacity. Mr Ward had no other general right to remuneration and, unless he could point to some provision in Guinness' articles entitling him to this sum as special remuneration, then he must be presumed to have acted gratuitously on Guinness' behalf.

Dorchester Finance Co Ltd v Stebbings (1977)

S, P and H were directors of the plaintiff company. S and P were chartered accountants and H had considerable accounting experience. The management of the company was left to S, with P and H fulfilling roles as non-executive directors. As neither P nor H visited the company frequently, they often left signed cheques in blank to be used by S at some later date. Losses were incurred when unsecured loans were made which turned out to be unrecoverable. The plaintiff company brought an action against S, P and H alleging negligence in the management of the company's affairs.

Held Foster J decided that all three were liable in negligence. A director in carrying out his duties was required to exhibit such a degree of skill as may reasonably be expected from a person of his knowledge and experience. No distinction was to be drawn between executive and non-executive directors. The court rejected the argument that non-executive directors could rely on the competence and diligence of the auditors and do nothing themselves, whether they had accounting experience or not.

Norman v Theodore Goddard (1991)

Q was a chartered surveyor with no knowledge of company law or offshore financial matters who was appointed as a director of LB Investments (LBI). B, a partner in Theodore Goddard, suggested that, for tax reasons, substantial sums held in cash by LBI should be invested in an offshore company. B made assurances to Q as to the profitability, availability and security of the funds. The offshore company was in fact controlled by B who stole the money transferred to it by LBI. Theodore Goddard sought a contribution from Q on the basis that he had acted in breach of his duty of care as a director of LBI.

Held Q was not in breach of duty and the claim of Theodore Goddard thus failed. The test of a director's duty was accurately stated in s 214(4) of the Insolvency Act 1986. The relevant test was what could be expected of a person in the position of director carrying out those functions. A director was entitled to trust persons in positions of responsibility until there was reason to distrust them.

Aberdeen Railway Co v Blaikie Bros (1854) HL

The appellant company agreed to buy goods from the respondent partnership. Blaikie was a member of the respondent partnership and was also a director of the appellant company. The company refused to honour the contract and the partnership sought its enforcement.

Held The House of Lords decided that the company was entitled to avoid the contract. There was a clear conflict between Blaikie's duty to secure for the company the lowest possible price, and his interest as a member of the partnership to make the greatest profit, and in such circumstances a contract was unenforceable against the company. Lord Cranworth stated: 'So strictly is this principle adhered to, that no question is allowed to be raised as to the fairness or unfairness of a contract so entered into.'

Heron International Ltd v Lord Grade (1983) CA

The directors of the target company of a proposed takeover were faced with two competing bids. The articles of the company gave the directors the power to choose which bid to accept. The directors, for a number of reasons, chose the lower bid. The plaintiffs, suing as representatives of the shareholders in the defendant company, sought an injunction to prevent the transfer.

Held The directors were under a fiduciary obligation to exercise the power to register a proposed transfer in the interests of both the company and the shareholders. The Court of Appeal decided that: 'Where directors have decided that it is in the best interests of a company that the company be taken over and there are two or more bidders the only duty of directors…is to obtain the best price.' In considering rival bids in a takeover the interests of the company were the interests of the current shareholders. The injunction was therefore granted.

Industrial Development Consultants Ltd v Cooley [1972] 2 All ER 162

The defendant was the managing director of the plaintiff company and had formerly been an architect with the West Midlands Gas Board. He entered into negotiations on behalf of the company with the Eastern Gas Board. Eastern

Gas informed the defendant that it would enter into the contract with him personally but not with the company. The defendant resigned as managing director of the company (on the pretext of ill health) in order to take up the Gas Board contract. The company sued for the profit made.

Held The defendant was liable for all benefits accruing under the contract, even though the plaintiff company had lost no corporate opportunity. Whilst managing director of the plaintiff company, a fiduciary relationship existed between himself and the company, and he was therefore under a duty to disclose all information revealed to him in the course of his dealings with the Gas Board. The defendant's actions had put his personal interest in direct conflict with the interests of the company, and this constituted a breach of his fiduciary duty for which he was accountable.

Re Barings plc (No 5) [2000] 1 BCLC 523, CA

The Court of Appeal, in upholding the disqualification order against a senior director of one of the Barings' group of companies, agreed with the following comments of Jonathan Parker J, the first instance judge:

1   Directors have, both collectively and individually, a continuing duty to acquire and maintain a sufficient knowledge and understanding of the company's business to enable them properly to discharge their duties as directors.

2   Whilst directors are entitled (subject to the articles of association of the company) to delegate particular functions to those below them in the management chain, and to trust their competence and integrity to a reasonable extent, the exercise of the power of delegation does not absolve a director from the duty to supervise the discharge of the delegated functions.

No rule of universal application can be formulated as to the duty referred to in (ii) above. The extent of the duty, and the question whether it has been discharged, must depend on the facts of each particular case, including the director's role in the management of the company.

Bradbury v English Sewing Cotton Co Ltd (1923) HL

The House of Lords examined the nature of shares and said that a share is a fractional part of the share capital. Shares are also the individual property of all the members but this does not mean that all the members as a group own the share capital. The share capital is something different from all the shares aggregated. The share capital belongs to the company.

Re William Leitch Brothers (No 1) (1932)

The company was incorporated in December 1926. By the end of 1929 the company was in serious financial difficulties, and by 30 March 1930 the company was unable to pay its debts. William Leitch, a director of the firm, knew that the company owed £6,500 and would not be able to pay it. However, he proceeded to borrow a further £6,000. In June of that year, the company was wound up and the liquidator wanted the court to find Mr Leitch personally liable for the debts of the company.

Held Mr Leitch was found guilty of fraudulent trading. The test should be subjective, that is, what was the knowledge of the particular director at the time? In other words, the court is not concerned with the question of what a,reasonable director would have believed had he been in the same position.

Re Patrick & Lyon Ltd (1933)

The case concerned the meaning of s 275 of the CA 1929 (now s213 IA 1986) which provided that:

If in the course of the winding up of a company it appears that any business of the company has been carried on with intent to defraud creditors of the company or...for any fraudulent purpose, the court, on the application of...the liquidator or any creditor or contributory...may declare that any of the directors...of the company who were knowingly parties to the carrying on of the business in manner aforesaid shall be personally responsible, without any limitation of liability, for all or any of the debts of the company as the court may direct.

That section was the forerunner of the modern s 216 of the lA 1986 and so what the court had to say then is still of relevance today.

Held The phrases 'intent to defraud' and 'fraudulent purpose' implied that actual dishonesty must be present as an element rather than fraud in the equitable sense. Maugham J said:

> [These] words connote actual dishonesty involving, according to current notions of fair trading among commercial men, real moral blame. No judge, I think, has ever been willing to define 'fraud' and I am attempting no definition.

Norman v Theodore Goddard (1991)

For facts, see 6.2 above. Hoffman J, in discussing a company director's common law duty of care and skill, said:

> ...a director performing active duties on behalf of the company need not exhibit a greater degree of skill than may rea-

sonably be expected from a person undertaking those duties. A director who undertakes the management of the company's properties is expected to have reasonable skill in property management, but not in offshore tax avoidance. It may be that in considering what a director ought reasonably to have known or inferred, one should also take into account the knowledge, skill and experience which he actually had in addition to that which a person carrying out his functions should be expected to have...

He went on to approve s214(4) of the IA 1986 as being an accurate statement of the extent of a director's duty of care and skill.

Re Maidstone Buildings Provisions Ltd (1971)

Mr Penney was the secretary for the company and not a director. Debts were incurred by the company when it was evident the company was insolvent.

Held The person concerned must take an active part in the fraudulent trading to be liable under this section. The fact that the secretary of the company warned the other directors that they should stop trading was not enough to render those directors liable for fraudulent trading.

Re Produce Marketing Consortium Ltd (No 2) (1989)

Two directors were running a fruit importing business and continued to do so when they ought to have known that there was no chance of the company remaining solvent.

Held They were liable under s 214 for wrongful trading. Although the two directors did not know that the company was in a grave financial situation and about to become insolvent, Knox J stated that that was immaterial. Under s 214 there is a objective test and the directors will be judged not just on what information they had but any information that, 'given reasonable diligence and an appropriate level of general knowledge, skill and experience, was ascertainable'.

Re DKG Contractors Ltd (1990)

Two directors of a groundwork company were consistently failing to have any regard to the Companies Acts, although they were never dishonest. The company then collapsed.

Held The directors were guilty of wrongful trading and had to contribute £500,000 towards the company's debts.

Levy v Abercorris Slate and Slab Co (1887)

The plaintiff's claim against the defendant was based upon an instrument that the defendant argued was void under the Bills of Sale Act (1878) Amendment Act 1882 whereas the plaintiff argued that it was a 'debenture' and therefore exempt from the strictures of that legislation. The court was therefore required to pronounce on the definition of 'debenture'.

Held Chitty J said that a debenture was a document which either created a debt or acknowledged it so that any document which fulfilled either of those conditions was a 'debenture'.

British India Steam Navigation Co v IRC (1881)

The company had issued instruments whereby the company promised to pay the holder of such an instrument £100 on 30 November 1882 and 5% interest half-yearly. The instruments were not under seal and in order to avoid a higher rate of stamp duty the company argued that they were not debentures but rather promissory notes.

Held The court disagreed. However, the court declined to ascribe a precise definition to the term debenture but made it clear it was capable of encompassing many different forms of instrument and an instrument not being under seal was no bar to its being a debenture.

Re Yorkshire Woolcombers Association Ltd (1903) CA

Romer LJ said that a floating charge had three key characteristics:

1   It is a charge on a class of assets of the company which includes present and future assets.

2   The composition of the class is not fixed—it changes from time to time in the ordinary course of the company's business.

The charge contemplates that the company is free to carry on business normally and deal with the assets subject to it in the ordinary course of that business until such time as the chargeholders enforce the charge—so it 'floats' in suspense until that time.

Aluminium Industrie Vaassen BV v Romalpa Aluminium Ltd (1976) CA

A Dutch company supplied aluminium foil to an English company. The contract between them contained a retention of title clause, which stated that legal title to the foil did not pass to the English company until full payment had been made. Anything made from the foil was to be held by the company as bailees and was to be kept separately from any other manufactured goods. The company was entitled to deal in the ordinary course of business with any products manufactured, but in such a case the company was acting as the agent of the supplier.

Held The clause was effective. The suppliers could claim any aluminium still in its original form, and they could trace into any proceeds of sale from goods manufactured from their aluminium.

Re Eric Holmes (1965)

A debenture in favour of Mr Richards was executed by the firm on 5 June. The documentation was sent to the company solicitors, but without a date on it. The solicitors were in a state of disarray at the time because the active partner had been killed. The date on the documentation was filled in as 23 June, which would have been within the 21 day period for registration. Evidently, if the true date of execution was used, the charge had not been registered within time. A certificate was issued by Companies House stating the requirements of the Act had been complied with.

Held The charge was valid. Section 98(2) of the CA 1948 (s401 of the CA 1985) states that a certificate is conclusive evidence that the requirements of the act have been complied with.

Re Telomatic (1994)

A charge was created by Barclays Bank over land owned by Telomatic. The charge was dated 4 January, but was not registered at Companies House at that time. The bank realised the charge had not been registered on 4 October and tried three times to procure security for their charge. On 5 October, the Cyprus Bank took a second charge over the property. Barclays Bank then applied to the court to get rectification of the register.

Held Registration out of time was not granted by the court. First, Barclays had misled the court as to,whether the company was to be wound up. Secondly, Barclays had tried to procure security in several ways before attempting to use s 404. Registration out of time will normally be granted, but it was held to be inequitable to do so in this instance.

Re Brightlife Ltd (1986)

Brightlife Ltd went into creditor's voluntary liquidation owing £200,000, secured by debenture to Norandex, and £70,000 to the Commissioners of Customs and Excise, who are classed as preferential creditors. A clause in the debenture stipulated that the chargee could crystallise the floating charge, if it was believed the security was in jeopardy. The liquidator wanted guidance as to the effectiveness of the clause.

Held The court stated that crystallisation was possible in this instance and consequently the debenture-holder did not have to wait until the preferential creditors were paid. Hoffman J was urged to consider the prejudice to other creditors that the operation of automatic crystallisation clauses could cause. However, he rejected this consideration saying:

> I do not think that it is open to the courts to restrict the contractual freedom of parties to a floating charge on such grounds. The floating charge was invented by Victorian lawyers to enable manufacturing and trading companies to raise loan capital on debentures. It could offer the security of a charge over the whole of the company's undertaking without inhibiting its ability to trade. But the mirror image of these advantages was the potential prejudice to the general body of creditors, who might know nothing of the floating charge but find that all the company's assets, including the very goods which they had just delivered on credit, had been swept up by the debenture-holder. The public interest requires a balancing of the advantages to the economy of facilitating the borrowing of money against the possibility of injustice to unsecured creditors. These arguments for and against floating charges are matters for Parliament rather than the courts...

Foss v Harbottle (1843)

The two plaintiffs, suing 'on behalf of themselves and all the other members of the corporation, except those who committed the injuries complained of' alleged that the defendants, who were the directors and promoters of the company, had, *inter alia,* sold land to the company at an undisclosed profit.

Held The individual minority shareholders were not the proper plaintiffs and could not therefore sue. If a wrong had been committed it had been committed against the company and therefore the proper plaintiff was the company. It was not open to individual members to assume to themselves the right of suing in the name of the company. Although this was a rule which could be departed from, it should not be, save for 'reasons of a very urgent character'. In the circumstances, there was not4ing to prevent the company from obtaining redress in its corporate character regarding the matters complained of.

Stein v Blake (1998) CA

The plaintiff owned half the shares in a number of companies. The defendant owned the other half and was sole director of the companies. It was alleged that the defendant had misappropriated assets from the companies and the plaintiff brought a personal claim against the defendant, claiming damages for the loss in value of his shares in the companies which had resulted from the misappropriation of the companies' assets. The companies were subsequently placed into liquidation, but no action was brought by the liquidators against the defendant.

Held The plaintiff could not recover from the defendant, as the loss caused to the plaintiff was only a reflection of the companies' loss and the companies were the proper plaintiffs to bring legal proceedings against the defendant. Millet LJ stated:

Directors owe fiduciary duties to their company to preserve and defend its assets and to the shareholders to advise them properly so that they are not induced or compelled to part with their shares at an undervalue. No doubt other fiduciary duties are also owed both to the company and to its shareholders. Shareholders may suffer loss in the event of a breach of either duty, but in the first case the loss consists of a diminution of the value of their shares, is fully reflected in the loss sustained by the company, and is fully compensated by restitution to the company. In the second case the company suffers no loss. Its assets are unaffected...All that is pleaded in the present case is wrongdoing to the company and loss suffered by the company. The only loss alleged to have been suffered by the plaintiff is reflected in the loss sustained by the company.

Ebrahimi v Westbourne Galleries (1973) HL

Ebrahimi and Nazar ran a successful carpet business as a partnership which they went on to incorporate. Nazar's son George was brought into the business and shares transferred to him. Friction occurred and Nazar and George excluded Ebrahimi from the business, removing him as a director. The profits of the business were paid out in the form of directors' salaries and not in dividends. Due to his exclusion, Ebrahimi saw none of the profits. He therefore petitioned for the company to be wound up on 'just and equitable' grounds.

Held The House of Lords unanimously granted the order for the company to be wound up. Lord Wilberforce defined the concept of 'just and equitable' as:

...a recognition of the fact that a limited company is more than a mere legal entity, with a personality in law of its own; that...there are individuals, with rights, expectations and obligations *inter se* which are not necessarily submerged in the company structure...It does, as equity always does, enable the court to subject the exercise of legal rights to equitable considerations, that is, of personal character arising between one individual and another, which may make it unjust or inequitable, to insist on legal rights, or to exercise them in a particular way.

His Lordship proceeded to set out some of the situations which he had in mind:

Sam Weller Ltd (1990)

The petitioners were the owners of around 43% of the issued share capital of a family company. The company was run by Sam Weller. In recent years, the company had become increasingly profitable. However, the dividend declared each year remained as it had done for the last 37 years. The petitioners alleged, *inter alia,* that the failure to approve the payment of larger dividends amounted to unfairly prejudicial conduct. Sam Weller applied to have the petition struck out by reason of the fact that the conduct alleged affected all members equally and could not therefore be unfairly prejudicial to the interests of some part of the members.

Held The application was dismissed because members might have different interests even if their rights as members were effectively the same. Conduct could be unfairly prejudicial within the meaning of s 459 notwithstanding that it affected all the members equally. Where conduct prejudiced all members equally, it could still be held to be unfairly prejudicial to the interests of some part of the members. The payment of low dividends was capable of amounting to conduct unfairly prejudicial to some of the members, including the petitioners.

Re Bird Precision Bellows Ltd (1984) CA

The petitioners had been directors until removed from office. They alleged that the company was in effect a quasi-partnership. Their removal was their wrongful exclusion from the conduct of the company's business. The petition under s 75 of the CA 1980 alleged that the affairs of the company had been conducted in a manner unfairly prejudicial to them, and requested that the respondents purchase the petitioners' shares.

Held The order was granted and the matter which arose was how to value the petitioners' shares. The court decided that if the sale was being forced because of the unfairly prejudicial conduct of the majority, and the shares had been acquired on the incorporation of a quasi-partnership company in which the petitioners had a legitimate expectation that they would participate, the price should be fixed on a *pro rata* basis. If the petitioners had conducted themselves so as to deserve exclusion from the company's affairs, the price should be discounted as if they had elected to sell their shares. In the instant case, the petitioners had been wrongfully excluded and thus the price should be fixed on a *pro rata* basis. The date for valuation was the date of the order.

Tesco Supermarkets Ltd v Nattrass (1972) HL

The appellant company was charged with an offence under the trade descriptions legislation of displaying inaccurate price information in one of its stores. The company was convicted and fined but appealed on the basis that the company had not committed the offence—it had in place a management and supervisory system designed to prevent this type of offence and the failure that resulted in the offence being committed was the failure of the store supervisor, which should not be attributed to the company.

Held The appeal succeeded. Because the store supervisory manager could not be said to be part of the 'directing mind and will' of the company his acts could not be said to be those of the company. The House of Lords stressed the fictional nature of the corporate legal person and the need to distinguish between:

- acts which were actually those of the company; and
- acts which were those of an agent or servant of the company but for which the company has some statutory or vicarious liability.

The former category are usually those acts committed by the board of directors or senior management of a company who speak and act for it. They are its 'brain' or its 'nerve centre'.

Director General of Fair Trading v Pioneer Concrete (UK) Ltd and Another (In Re Supply of Ready Mixed Concrete (No 2)) (1995) HL

The respondent companies had, at a senior level put in place compliance systems to ensure that no employee breached injunctions restraining contravention of restrictive trade practices legislation. Contrary to the companies' express instructions and without their knowledge, some of the employees went ahead and ignored the injunctions. The companies argued that they should not be vicariously liable for the acts of these employees as they acted without any form of authority and contrary to explicit instructions. The court at first instance disagreed and held the companies to be nonetheless in contempt of court. The Court of Appeal allowed the companies' appeal and the Director General of Fair Trading, who is responsible for the enforcement of restrictive practices legislation, appealed to the House of Lords.

Held The appeal was allowed. Since a company is a fictional person, it can only act through the medium of its agents and the actions of its employees acting in the course of their employment amount to the carrying on of business by the company. Simply because a prohibition at senior level existed, designed to prevent illegal agreements being made, it was not enough to prevent the companies becoming party to such agreements where the prohibition was ignored by the employees. Lord Templeman said that 'an employee who acts for the company within the scope of his employment is the company. Directors may give instructions, top management may exhort, middle management may question and workers may listen attentively. But if a worker makes a defective product or a lower manager accepts or rejects an order, he is the company'.

Lennard's Carrying Co Ltd v Asiatic Petroleum Co Ltd (1915) HL

The appellants were ship owners and one of their ships caught fire due to its unseaworthy condition, destroying its cargo. When sued by the cargo owners the appellants relied on the statutory let out in the Merchant Shipping Act 1894 that they would not be liable for damages to cargo owners where the loss occurred without their 'actual fault or privity'. The managing director of the appellant company was in full control of the management of the ship.
Held Because of the position he enjoyed, the acts of the managing director in managing the ship could be seen as the acts of the company. The appellant company was responsible for his acts and defaults and so the company could not escape liability by relying on the statutory defence.

Attorney General's Reference (No 2 of 1982) (2984) CA

The defendant had been charged with theft from companies of which they were sole directors and shareholders. They had been acquitted following *Tesco Supermarkets v Nattrass,* the sole owners of a company were its directing mind and will and therefore could not be said to steal from it.
Held The judge's interpretation of *Tesco Supermarkets* was wrong—that case's reasoning related to the company as perpetrator not victim of offences. Where all the members/directors, even if they are sole controllers of a company, act illegally and dishonestly appropriate that company's property they can be said to be guilty of theft.

Business Names Act 1985

1   Persons subject to this Act

(1) This Act applies to any person who has a place of business in Great Britain and who carries on business in Great Britain under a name which—

(a) in the case of a partnership, does not consist of the surnames of all part-ners who are individuals and the corporate names of all partners who are bodies corporate without any addition other than an addition permitted by this Act;

(b) in the case of an individual, does not consist of his surname without any addition other than one so permitted;

(c) in the case of a company, being a company which is capable of being wound up under the Companies Act 1985, does not consist of its corpo-rate name without any addition other than one so permitted;

(d) in the case of a limited liability partnership, does not consist of its corpo-rate name without any addition other than one so permitted.

(2) The following are permitted additions for the purposes of subsection (1)—

(a) in the case of a partnership, the forenames of individual partners or the initials of those forenames or, where two or more individual partners have the same surname, the addition of "s" at the end of that surname; or

(b) in the case of an individual, his forename or its initial;

(c) in any case, any addition merely indicating that the business is carried on in succession to a former owner of the business.

2 Prohibition of use of certain business names

(1) Subject to the following subsections, a person to whom this Act applies shall not, without the written approval of the Secretary of State, carry on business in Great Britain under a name which—

(a) would be likely to give the impression that the business is connected with Her Majesty's Government[, with any part of the Scottish Administration,] or with any local authority; or

(b) includes any word or expression for the time being specified in regula-tions made under this Act.

(2) Subsection (1) does not apply to the carrying on of a business by a per-son—

(a) to whom the business has been transferred on or after 26th February 1982; and

(b) who carries on the business under the name which was its lawful business name immediately before that transfer, during the period of 12 months beginning with the date of that transfer.

(3) Subsection (1) does not apply to the carrying on of a business by a person who—

(a) carried on that business immediately before 26th February 1982; and

(b) continues to carry it on under the name which immediately before that date was its lawful business name.

(4) A person who contravenes subsection (1) is guilty of an offence.

3   Words and expressions requiring Secretary of State's approval

(1) The Secretary of State may by regulations—

(a) specify words or expressions for the use of which as or as part of a business name his approval is required by section 2(1)(b); and

(b) in relation to any such word or expression, specify a Government department or other body as the relevant body for purposes of the following subsection.

(2) Where a person to whom this Act applies proposes to carry on a business under a name which is or includes any such word or expression, and a Government department or other body is specified under subsection (1)(b) in relation to that word or expression, that person shall—

(a) request (in writing) the relevant body to indicate whether (and if so why) it has any objections to the proposal; and

(b) submit to the Secretary of State a statement that such a request has been made and a copy of any response received from the relevant body.

4   Disclosure required of persons using business names

(1) A person to whom this Act applies shall—

(a) [subject to subsections (3) and (3A)], state in legible characters on all business letters, written orders for goods or services to be supplied to the business, invoices and receipts issued in the course of the business and written demands for payment of debts arising in the course of the business—

(i) in the case of a partnership, the name of each partner,

(ii) in the case of an individual, his name,

(iii) in the case of a company, its corporate name,...

(iiia) In the case of a limited liability partnership, its corporate name and the name of each member, and

(iv) in relation to each person so named, an address in Great Britain at which service of any document relating in any way to the business will be effective; and

(b) in any premises where the business is carried on and to which the customers of the business or suppliers of any goods or services to the business have access, display in a prominent position so that it may easily be read by such customers or suppliers a notice containing such names and addresses.

(2) A person to whom this Act applies shall secure that the names and addresses required by subsection (1)(a) to be stated on his business letters, or which would have been so required but for subsection (3) or (3A), are immediately given, by written notice to any person with whom anything is done or discussed in the course of the business and who asks for such names and addresses.

(3) Subsection (1)(a) does not apply in relation to any document issued by a partnership of more than 20 persons which maintains at its principal place of business a list of the names of all the partners if—

(a) none of the names of the partners appears in the document otherwise than in the text or as a signatory; and

(b) the document states in legible characters the address of the partnership's principal place of business and that the list of the partners' names is open to inspection at that place.

(3A) Subsection (1)(a) does not apply in relation to any document issued by a limited liability partnership with more than 20 members which maintains at its principal place of business a list of the names of all the members if—

(a) none of the names of the members appears in the document otherwise than in the text or as a signatory; and

(b) the document states in legible characters the address of the principal place of business of the limited liability partnership and that the list of the members' names is open to inspection at that place.]

(4) Where a partnership maintains a list of the partners' names for purposes of subsection (3), any person may inspect the list during office hours.

(4A) Where a limited liability partnership maintains a list of the members' names for the purposes of subsection (3A), any person may inspect the list during office hours.

(5) The Secretary of State may by regulations require notices under subsection (1)(b) or (2) to be displayed or given in a specified form.

(6) A person who without reasonable excuse contravenes subsection (1) or (2), or any regulations made under subsection (5), is guilty of an offence.

(7) Where an inspection required by a person in accordance with subsection (4) or (4A) is refused, any partner of the partnership concerned, or any member of the limited liability partnership concerned, who without reasonable excuse refused that inspection, or permitted it to be refused, is guilty of an offence.

5 Civil remedies for breach of s 4

(1) Any legal proceedings brought by a person to whom this Act applies to enforce a right arising out of a contract made in the course of a business in respect of which he was, at the time the contract was made, in breach of subsection (1) or (2) of section 4 shall be dismissed if the defendant (or, in Scotland, the defender) to the proceedings shows—

(a) that he has a claim against the plaintiff (pursuer) arising out of that contract which he has been unable to pursue by reason of the latter's breach of section 4(1) or (2), or

(b) that he has suffered some financial loss in connection with the contract by reason of the plaintiff's (pursuer's) breach of section 4(1) or (2),

unless the court before which the proceedings are brought is satisfied that it is just and equitable to permit the proceedings to continue.

(2) This section is without prejudice to the right of any person to enforce such rights as he may have against another person in any proceedings brought by that person.

6 Regulations

(1) Regulations under this Act shall be made by statutory instrument and may contain such transitional provisions and savings as the Secretary of State thinks appropriate, and may make different provision for different cases or classes of case.

(2) In the case of regulations made under section 3, the statutory instrument containing them shall be laid before Parliament after the regulations are made and shall cease to have effect at the end of the period of 28 days beginning with the day on which they were made (but without prejudice to anything previously done by virtue of them or to the making of new regulations) unless during that period they are approved by a resolution of each House of Parliament.

In reckoning this period of 28 days, no account is to be taken of any time during which Parliament is dissolved or prorogued, or during which both Houses are adjourned for more than 4 days.

(3) In the case of regulations made under section 4, the statutory instrument containing them is subject to annulment in pursuance of a resolution of either House of Parliament.

7   Offences

(1) Offences under this Act are punishable on summary conviction.

(2) A person guilty of an offence under this Act is liable to a fine not exceeding one-fifth of the statutory maximum.

(3) If after a person has been convicted summarily of an offence under section 2 or 4(6) the original contravention is continued, he is liable on a second or subsequent summary conviction of the offence to a fine not exceeding one-fiftieth of the statutory maximum for each day on which the contravention is continued (instead of to the penalty which may be imposed on the first conviction of the offence).

(4) Where an offence under section 2 or 4(6) or (7) committed by a body corporate is proved to have been committed with the consent or connivance of, or to be attributable to any neglect on the part of, any director, manager, secretary or other similar officer of the body corporate, or any person who was purporting to act in any such capacity, he as well as the body corporate is guilty of the offence and liable to be proceeded against and punished accordingly.

(5) Where the affairs of a body corporate are managed by its members, subsection (4) applies in relation to the acts and defaults of a member in connection with his functions of management as if he were a director of the body corporate.

(6) For purposes of the following provisions of the Companies Act 1985 —

(a) section 731 (summary proceedings under the Companies Acts), and

(b) section 732(3) (legal professional privilege),

this Act is to be treated as included in those Acts.

8   Interpretation

(1) The following definitions apply for purposes of this Act—

"business" includes a profession;

"initial" includes any recognised abbreviation of a name;

"lawful business name", in relation to a business, means a name under which the business was carried on without contravening section 2(1) of this Act or section 2 of the Registration of Business Names Act 1916;

"local authority" means any local authority within the meaning of the Local Government Act 1972 or the Local Government (Scotland) Act 1973, the Common Council of the City of London or the Council of the Isles of Scilly;

"partnership" includes a foreign partnership;

and "surname", in relation to a peer or person usually known by a British title different from his surname, means the title by which he is known.

(2) Any expression used in this Act and also in the Companies Act 1985 has the same meaning in this Act as in that.

9   Northern Ireland

This Act does not extend to Northern Ireland.

10   Commencement

This Act comes into force on 1st July 1985.

11   Citation

This Act may be cited as the Business Names Act 1985.

CONSUMER PROTECTION

The basics

In the area of consumer protection, there is, on the one hand, the sanctity of freedom of contract and the right of tradesmen and retailers to get the best deal they can with the consuming public and, on the other hand, there is the need to protect the public from defective products, unfair advertising and agreements which are too heavily based in favour of the retailer.

Certain types of transactions are entered into by consumers every day, eg. the shopper visiting the supermarket to buy groceries, the handyman at the DIY shop or car accessory shop, the child buying sweets, even. They all enter into contracts for the sale and supply of goods.

However, consumers may wish to acquire goods but do not have the immediate finance to pay for them. Hire-purchase and other forms of credit are an important form of consumer transactions.

Contracts for the sale of goods

These contracts contain express and implied conditions and warranties which are referred to as the terms of the contract. They set out the rights and obligations of the parties under the contract, for example in the Sale of Goods Act 1979.

The Sale of Goods Act 1979

This 1979 Act implies terms into contracts for the sale of goods. The SOG Act deals mainly with rules governing the parties' obligations to each other and the transfer of ownership of the goods. Contracts of sale are usually made without need for any legal requirements, eg, cash sale of goods in shops or food and drink sold in a restaurant.

The contract of sale is defined as "a contract whereby the seller transfers or agrees to transfer the property in the goods to the buyer for a money consideration called the price."

This covers

1. a sale—where ownership of the goods passes immediately to the buyer when he tenders the price;

2. an agreement to sell—where the parties agree that ownership is to pass in the future.

With certain exceptions the parties are free to make whatever sort of contract they wish. The obligations under the contract are largely a matter for the parties themselves to decide. In the absence of such express agreement the Act implies certain obligations.

The right to sell the goods

The implied terms form the cornerstone of consumer protection in the civil law. (section 12–15 Sale of Goods Act 1979).

Section 12 is concerned with the right of the seller to sell the goods. This is a central part of the contract.

Section 12(1) SOG Act states "there is an implied condition on the part of the seller that in the case of a sale, he has the right to sell the goods, and in the case of an agreement to sell, he will have such a right at the time when the property is to pass."

So, if a seller has no right to sell the goods, because, eg, they are stolen, he is in breach of this condition under the Act.

Description of the goods

There is an implied requirement that the goods will correspond with any description applied to them. Section 13(1) Sale Of Goods Act states that "where there is a contract for the sale of goods by description there is an implied condition that the goods shall correspond with that description".

This applies to goods that are ordered from catalogues and brochures and to descriptions on the packaging of articles. There is a breach, for example, if the box refers to a blue double-sized electric blanket and when it is opened, it contains a pink single-sized blanket. (see the case-law <u>Beale v Taylor [1967]</u>). But there needs to be a sale by description. (see the case-law <u>Leinster Enterprises Ltd v Christopher Hull Fine Art Ltd [1990]</u>).

Quality and fitness for purpose

If there is a business sale, ie, between a retailer and a private individual, there is an implied condition as to quality and fitness for purpose.

Section 14(2) Sale of Goods Act implies a term that where goods are sold in the course of a business, the goods must be of a satisfactory quality.

Section 14(2)(A) provides that the goods are of a satisfactory quality if they meet the standard that a reasonable person would regard as satisfactory, taking account of any description of the goods, the price and other relevant circumstances.

Section 14(2)(B) states that the following are, in appropriate cases, aspects of the quality of the goods:
- fitness for all the purposes for which the goods of the kind in question are commonly supplied
- appearance and finish
- freedom from minor defects
- safety
- durability

Sale by sample

Section 15(1) Sale of Goods Act provides that "where goods are sold by sample, the bulk shall correspond with the sample and the buyer shall have a reasonable opportunity of comparing the bulk with the sample. Further, that the goods will be free from any defect which would make their quality unsatisfactory and which would not be apparent upon a reasonable examination of the sample."

This section applies, for example, to wallpaper, curtain material, or a suit which may be ordered after looking at a retailer's pattern books. (Godfrey v Perry [1960]).

Ownership and risk

Apart from implying terms into contracts for the sale of goods, the Sale of Goods Act also provides for other matters, such as the passage of the owner-ship of and the risk attached to the goods.

In a contract for the sale of goods it is important to know when the property in the goods passes from the seller to the buyer. With the passing of the property often goes the passing of the risk of the goods being destroyed or damaged. Generally if the contract refers to a specific item, the property passes as soon as the contract is made. If however, modifications have to be made to the goods, the property passes only when this has been done and the buyer has been noti-fied to this effect.

If the buyer takes goods on approval, the property only passes to the buyer when he signifies to the seller his intention to keep the goods. If goods have not been set aside or specifically assigned to the buyer then property only passes to the buyer when this process has been completed.

The rights of the parties

Once a contract for the sale of goods has been made, the seller is under an obli-gation to deliver the goods. This can mean actual delivery or the buyer can be handed the means of access to the goods, eg, the keys to a warehouse where the goods are stored. If the seller refuses to deliver the goods, the buyer can either sue for damages for any loss incurred by him arising out of refusal, or, obtain an order for specific performance.

If the seller delivers the wrong goods then the buyer can accept or reject them as he sees fit. This right to reject the goods is very important for the buyer. If the goods do not match their description, or are not of satisfactory quality, then his delivery cannot be a delivery of the correct goods, and the buyer can reject them. However, this right to reject can be lost. It is lost where the buyer has accepted the goods.(section 11(2)). But acceptance (section 35) does not always mean saying that the goods are all right. It can mean saying nothing—failing to exercise the right to reject the goods for beyond a "reasonable time". (Bernstein v Pamsons Motors [1986]).

If the buyer refuses wrongfully to accept delivery of the correct goods, then he can be sued by the seller for damages. If the ownership of the goods has passed to the buyer and he refuses to pay, then he can be sued for the price of the goods.

The Sale of Goods Act, section 19, allows a seller to "reserve the right of disposal" of the goods.

CONSUMER CREDIT

Consumer credit encompasses the financing of consumer transactions.
The Consumer Credit Act 1974 is the requisite piece of legislation that you need to understand.

A BILL OF EXCHANGE

A bill of exchange is defined in section 3 of the Bills of Exchange Act 1882 as "an unconditional order in writing, addressed by one person to another, signed by the person giving it, requiring the person to whom it is addressed to pay on demand or at a fixed or determinable future time a sum certain in money to or to the other of a specified person, or to bearer"

Section 31 of Bills of Exchange Act 1882
"A BILL is negotiated when it is transferred from one person to another in such a manner
as to constitute the transferee the holder of the BILL. A BILL payable to order is negotiated by the endorsement of the holder and is completed by delivery.

Section 32 of the BILLS of Exchange Act 1882 states that:

(i) An endorsement must be written on the bill itself and signed by the endorser. The simple signature of the endorser is sufficient; if a copy of the bill is legally recognised, any endorsement written on a copy of a bill is deemed to be written on the bill itself.

(ii) It must be endorsement of the whole bill. There cannot be an endorsement which transfers only part of the amount payable or which purports to transfer the bill to two or more endorsees.

(iii) If there are two or more payees or endorsers who are not partners, they must all endorse the bill; unless the one endorsing has authority to endorse for the others.

(iv) Where a bill is payable to order, if the name of a payee or endorsee is wrongly designated or is mis-spelt, etc the endorser must add his or her proper signature.

(v) If there are two or more endorsements on a bill they are deemed to have been made in the order in which they appear on the bill.

An endorsement may be in blank where an endorser merely adds his or her signature to the bill. The bill then becomes a "BEARER BILL" under section 34(1) Bills of Exchange Act 1882. It authorises payment to anyone to whom the bill is delivered.

Under section 55(2), the effect of endorsement is that the endorser is promising that when the bill is presented it will be accepted and paid, and in the event of dishonour he or she will compensate the holder or any subsequent endorser who is compelled to pay. Therefore a valid endorsement is an essential link in the chain of ownership of a bill of exchange.

CHEQUES

are negotiable instruments and become payable on demand as part of the relationship between banker and customer.

Under section 73 of the Bills of Exchange Act 1882, they can be negotiated in the same way as other negotiable instruments.

CUSTOMERS AND BANKS

The relation between a banker and his customer is one of DEBTOR and CREDITOR.

It is a relationship founded in contract.

The word "CUSTOMER" is NOT defined by law but at common law a customer is someone who has an account in his own name at a bank.

The customer has duties as per the bank agreement:

1. A duty to of care to the bank NOT to draw up cheques carelessly. This limits fraud and forgery. (London Joint Stock Bank v Macmillan and Arthur [1918]).

2. A customer is under a duty to inform the bank of forgeries. If a customer fails in this duty he may be estopped from denying the validity of the forged signature.(Greenwood v Martin's Bank [1933])

DUTIES OWED BY THE BANK

1. To pay money to the order of the customer. The bank must honour cheques or other orders drawn on the customer's account, provided that the account has sufficient funds or is within an agreed overdraft limit. This is the bank's primary duty. (Tassell v Cooper [1850]).

A cheque returned with the wording 'refer to drawer' may leave the bank open to a claim of defamation if they failed to honour it when sufficient funds have been present in the account.

2. The bank has the duty to keep the affairs of the customer secret. (Tournier v National Provincial and Union Bank of England[1924]).

3. The bank has the duty to keep customers informed about their financial position. As part of the duty the bank must maintain the customer's account correctly. If the customer is misled by an inaccurate statement of his or her account, and acts upon this irregularly, the bank will be unable to recover any money that has been wrongly credited. (United Overseas Bank v Jiwani[1976])

CONSUMER CREDIT AGREEMENT

The Consumer Credit Act 1974 applies primarily to regulated agreements as defined in the Act. A consumer credit agreement is defined as 'an agreement by which the creditor provides an individual (the debtor) with credit not exceeding a specified sum'—at present £25,000.00.

Where the debtor is a company or other body corporate, an agreement is NOT a consumer credit agreement. It is a contract. The debtor of a consumer credit agreement MUST be a natural person, an individual, and credit must be granted in the course of business.

A regulated consumer hire agreement is defined as 'an agreement made between a person and the hirer under which goods are hired, leased or bailed and which is capable of lasting more than 3 months and does not require the hirer to make payments exceeding £25,000.00 (section 15).

Short term hire agreements, eg, the daily hire of DIY tools are excluded. But a short term hire with a provision for renewal may fall within the definition as it may be capable of lasting more than 3 months.

Credit—Token Agreements

Credit token agreements may also be regulated agreements. These are defined in section 14 of the Act as 'a card, voucher, cheque, coupon, stamp, form, booklet or other document or thing given to an individual by a person carrying on a consumer credit business, who undertakes

a) that on the production of it he will supply goods, cash and services on credit, or

b) that where on the production of it to a third party, the third party supplies cash, goods and services, he will pay the third party for them, in return for payment to him by the individual.

Examples of credit tokens are in-store credit cards and bank credit cards.

The Hire Purchase Agreement is defined as an agreement under which

a) goods are hired in return for periodic payments by the person to whom they are hired (the debtor);

b) the ownership of the goods will pass to the debtor if the terms of the agreement are complied with and one or more of the following occur :-

(i) the exercise of an option to purchase by the debtor;

(ii) the doing of any other specified act by any party to the agreement;

(iii) the happening of any other specified event.

There is a clear distinction between hire purchase agreements and conditional sale agreements. Conditional sale agreement commits a buyer to purchase.

Hire purchase agreements do not commit the hirer to purchase. Conditional sale agreements are agreements for the sale of goods or land under which the purchase price is payable by instalments and ownership of the goods or land is retained by the seller, in spite of the fact that the buyer is in possession of them, until such conditions as to the payment of instalments, etc, as specified in the agreement are fulfilled.9section 189) The Consumer Credit Act 1974 contains provisions which apply exclusively to these two types of agreement, such as the debtor's statutory right to terminate under section 99.

There are also provisions which bring small agreements within the Act. Small agreements may be either a regulated agreement where, with respect to the former, the amount of credit does not exceed £50 and with respect to the latter, the hire/rental charge does not exceed £50. The rules for determining whether the credit exceeds the limit are explained by reference to fixed-sum and running-account credit. Small agreements are exempt from some of the provision of the Act, such as those relating to unsolicited credit tokens. Section 51). The main provisions contained in Part IV of the Act relating to seeking business, the requirement on the creditor to supply information on request and the provisions restricting remedies on default, will apply.

Certain types of agreement are exempted from the provisions of the Consumer Credit Act 1974, section 16, for example, mortgages or any loan made by banks, building societies, local authorities, etc. for the buying or developing of land; credit agreements in respect of the export and import of goods; normal trade credit—where credit is provided in the sale of goods and services but the "bill" is to be paid as one single instalment, for example milk or paper bill and the hiring of meters/equipment from the essential services, gas, electricity and telecommunications service.

Non-commercial agreements are also exempt from some of the provisions of the Consumer Credit Act 1974. Such agreements are made by a creditor not in the course of a business carried on (section 189). Non-commercial agreements are exempt from formal documentary requirements, cancellation rights, cooling-off periods, the duty to supply information and the licensing provisions.

Regulated agreements can be sub-categorised into debtor-creditor-supplier agreements. This is a restricted use consumer credit agreement where the creditor and supplier are either the same person, eg. financing purchase by the customer, or there are pre-existing arrangements between the creditor and the supplier, eg. credit card transactions. In this kind of agreement the debtor can bring an action against the creditor for any misrepresentation or breach of contract on the part of the supplier 9section 75)Another example of restricted agreements are the debtor-creditor agreements. The debtor-creditor agreement is defined as any agreement not falling within the definition of a debtor-creditor-supplier agreement. If an agreement falls within more than one

category it will be known as a multiple agreement and each divisible part will be regulated accordingly. The difference between a debtor-creditor agreement and a debtor-creditor-supplier agreement is that in the latter, both the creditor and the supplier may become liable to the debtor for defects in the goods.
Another type of regulated agreement is the unrestricted-use credit agreement where the debtor has no control over the use to which the credit is put.

Another type of regulated agreement is the restricted use credit agreement where the debtor has control over the use of the finance.

Legislation
A contract of hire-purchase of goods embodies statutory implied terms which may not be excluded in consumer transactions (sections 8–10 Sale of Goods Act 1973)

Right to sell
There is an implied condition that the creditor will have the right to sell the goods at the time property is to pass (section 8(1)(a) Sale of Goods Act 1973) whether or not that is the purpose for which goods are commonly supplied.

Enforcement of a regulated agreement
Where the creditor is required to apply to the court for an order to enforce a regulated agreement, eg. under section 65(1) of the Consumer Credit Act 1974 and the agreement was properly executed, the court:

a) may reduce or discharge any sum payable by the debtor or hirer to compensate for prejudice suffered as a result of the contravention (section 127(2) CCA 1974);

b) may make a time order under section 129 CCA 1974;

c) may discuss the application if it considers it just to do so, having regard to the prejudice caused and the degree of culpability for the contravention and its powers under sections 135 and 136 CCA 1974 to impose conditions on any order or to vary the terms of the agreement (section 127(1) CCA 1974);

d) must dismiss the application where there was non-compliance with:

   (i) section 61(a)CCA 1974 requiring the debtor personally and the creditor or hirer, to sign the agreement; or

   (ii) in the case of a cancellable agreement, sections 62 and 63 CCA 1974 requiring the supply of copies of the agreement to the debtor or hirer or section 64(1) CCA 1974 requiring notice of cancellation rights to be given (section 127(3) and (4) CCA 1974).

Note that this total bar to enforcement imposed by the terms of (I) above contravene Human Rights Act 1998, right to a fair trial in that the lender is deprived of a fair and public hearing, and because the lender is

improperly deprived of his possessions in that he is unable to enjoy benefits from the contractual rights arising from the loan agreement, or the rights arising from the delivery of the goods given as security. (Wilson v First County Trust [2001] CA)

But the above provisions remain in force until the CCA 1974 is amended.

PROTECTION BEFORE YOU MAKE THE AGREEMENT

Regulations in section 55 to 59 of the Consumer Credit Act 1974 requires that you disclose specified information in a prescribed manner to the debtor or hirer before a regulated agreement is made. Failure to comply with such regulations results in an agreement being improperly executed and enforceable against the debtor or hirer only be court order.

As long as the regulated agreement has NOT been concluded, the intended debtor or hirer may withdraw by giving written or oral notice evidencing his intention to do so to the creditor or owner, or:

(i) to the credit-broker or supplier who is the negotiator, or

(ii) to any person, who in the course of business, acts on behalf of the debtor or hirer in any negotiations for the agreement.

Such persons are deemed to be the agent of the creditor or owner for this purpose.

DISCLOSURE

Section 157 CCA 1974 states that the creditor must disclose to the hirer any credit references he has consulted as to the hirer's credit-worthiness. He must disclose that he has done so within 7 days of doing so. The creditor must also give individuals a statement of their consumer agreement rights. It is an offence not to do so.

CANCELLATION

The relevant legislation is section 67-73 CCA 1974. An agreement is cancellable where:

(i) oral representations are made in prior negotiations in the presence of the debtor or hirer, or

(ii) the debtor or hirer signs other than at the place of business of the creditor or hirer, negotiator or party to a linked transaction (s 67 CCA 1974)

The only exceptions are when LAND is being hired and when the agreement is for a bridging loan to finance the purchase of land. The debtor or hirer can cancel the agreement by giving notice of his cancellation within 5 working days following the day of receipt of the cancellation.

When a regulated agreement is cancelled, any linked transaction is also cancelled and any money paid by the debtor or hirer becomes repayable and part-exchange goods must be returned or an allowance paid.
Any credit provided to the debtor under a consumer credit agreement is to be repaid within one month.

The Consumer Protection Act 1987

A consumer who can establish that a defendant produced (or imported into the European Community) the product which caused his injury because it was defective, can claim under the Consumer Protection Act. This Act combines contract law, tort of negligence and protection for third parties and bystanders.

The Consumer Credit Act 1974

The aim of this statute is to provide reasonable protection for consumers. It does this in the following ways:

- it regulates the formation, terms and enforcement of credit agreements;

- anyone engaged in consumer credit business must be licensed to carry on the business;

- an advertisement for credit must show the true cost of the credit;

- restrictions are placed on door-to-door selling on credit;

- it creates criminal offences, eg, trading without the necessary licence.

The Act applies to consumer credit agreements. These are defined in section 8 as credit agreements made between an individual and any other person by which the creditor provides the debtor with credit not exceeding £15,000. The term "individual" includes partnerships and unincorporated bodies but not companies.

Credit agreements include hire-purchase agreements, conditional sale agreements, credit sale agreements, loan agreements, and bank overdraft agreements.

The Consumer Credit Act 1974 is a long and complicated statute.

The Trade Descriptions Act 1968

It is an offence under this Act for any person, in the course of trade or business:

- to apply a false trade description to goods (section!);
- to supply, or offer to supply, goods with such a description (sect.1); or
- knowingly or recklessly to make a false statement as to the provision of any services, accommodation or facilities (sect.14).

A false trade description

A trade description is an indication of any of the following:

- quantity, size or gauge;
- method of manufacture, production, etc;
- fitness for purpose, strength, performance, behaviour or accuracy;
- physical characteristics not included above;
- testing and results thereof;
- approval by any person or conformity with an approved type;
- place or date of manufacture, production, etc;
- person by whom manufactured, produced, etc;
- other history, including previous ownership or use.

The description must be "false to a material degree". This means that it must be capable of inducing the sale or supply of the goods. The meaning to be attributed to the description is essentially decided by considering its likely effect on the ordinary man, eg, a "beautiful" car has been held to indicate both its appearance and its running order.

Oral representations, advertisements, mileometer readings, are all capable of being trade descriptions.

<u>Sale or supply</u>

The offence under section 1 Trade Descriptions Act is committed either by applying the false trade description of goods, or supplying, or offering to supply goods to which such a description has been applied.

<u>False statements as to services</u>

There can be no liability under section 14 of the Act unless, at the time the statement was made, it was false and the defendant knew it, or was reckless as to whether it was false.

<u>Defences</u>

As regards section 1, a defence would be if the trader had indicated by a disclaimer that the consumer should place no reliance on the trade description. As regards section 14, the trader can defend himself(section 24) if he can prove that the offence was caused by:

- mistake
- reliance on information supplied to him
- the act or default of another person
- an accident
- some other cause beyond his control, and in any event, that he took all reasonable precautions and exercised all due diligence to avoid the commission of the offence by himself or any other person under his control.

The Consumer Protection Act 1987

Part 2 of this Act empowers the Secretary of State to make regulations concerning the safe design, construction, manufacture, assembly and packaging of products. Its aim is to try to ensure that consumer products are designed and built to high safety standards.

The marketing of unsafe products may be prevented by the Secretary of State issuing:

1. a prohibition notice, which is a particular ban relating only to the trader upon whom it is served.

2. a notice to warn, which applies to the particular trader served and, unlike the above, concerns goods which he has already supplied. The notice can require the trader to publish a warning about unsafe products, eg, an advertisement warning purchasers of a particular make of car that it has defective brakes which should be checked by the dealer.

Contravention of safety regulations or a notice to warn is a crime. A an injured party may bring an action for damages against a trader who has infringed a safety regulation or a prohibition order.

The Unsolicited Goods and Services Act 1971

This statute is designed to prevent inertia selling., ie, unordered goods sent to the consumer with the implication that he is expected to pay for them. The Act provides that six months after such receipt, the goods are deemed to belong unconditionally to the recipient. If the recipient does not want to wait six months, he may send a written notice to the sender asking him to remove the goods. If thirty days lapse and the goods are not removed, they belong to the recipient.

The Act also contains criminal sanctions which are confined to persons acting in the course of a trade or business. It is an offence for such persons to demand payment for unsolicited goods without reasonably believing in a right to payment. In such cases it is also an offence to assert a right to payment, to threaten legal proceedings, to place or threaten to place the consumer's name on a default list or to invoke or threaten to invoke any other collection procedure.

The Data Protection Act 1998

The Data Protection Act requires that appropriate security measures are in place to safeguard against unauthorised or unlawful access/processing of personal data. The data must be processed lawfully, obtained and used on specified lawful purposes, must be relevant and not excessive. The data must be kept no longer than necessary, kept secure.

Since the Data Protection Act, there came into being the Employment Practices Data Protection Code, of which the third part was published in June 2003. The Code aims to help employers comply with the Data Protection Act 1998 when processing employees' personal data. The last part (3) focuses on the steps employers must take to comply with the Act when monitoring their staff.

The Code describes monitoring as "activities that set out to collect information about workers by keeping them under some sort of observation", whether directly or through the use of electronic systems. Such monitoring may be routine, adopted for all or some workers as a matter of course, or one-off and introduced in response to a particular problem. Both types of monitoring are covered by the Code if a manual record is made or automated processing is carried out. Reviewing a log of websites visited by employees, accessing employee voicemails and checking e-mail accounts can all amount to monitoring.

The Code is likely to apply if the purpose of monitoring is to check the performance or conduct of employees. The Code does not cover access to records kept in the normal course of business that are accessed only in response to a particular concern or query, such as a customer complaint. For example, reviewing an employee's email account in response to pending or threatened litigation should not be covered by the Code.

New development on Data Protection Act

Impact assessments

If monitoring is carried out to assess conduct or performance, the key to complying with the Act will be to do an impact assessment before monitoring starts. An impact assessment involves balancing the employer's interest in the proposed monitoring with the possible prejudice to the employee, before deciding whether monitoring is justified.

The Code outlines a 5 step process:

1. Identify the purpose of the monitoring and likely benefits for the business.
2. Identify any adverse impact the monitoring will have both for employees and customers.
3. Consider whether the same benefits can be achieved in a different, less intrusive way.
4. The employer will have obligations to staff as a result of monitoring. Employees should be notified about the monitoring that is being conducted.
5. Balancing these factors will help the employer to take the decision about whether the proposed monitoring is justified. The Code stresses that fairness to employees is the most important factor.

The Code contains a series of good practice recommendations for employers to adopt in monitoring staff. Covert monitoring will only be justified in exceptional circumstances, such as suspected criminal activity or other malpractice, where notifying staff about the monitoring would prejudice the ability of an employer to detect the conduct of the employee.

Conclusion on Consumer Law

In the area of consumer protection, there is the sanctity of freedom of contract on the one hand and the right of businesses to get the best deal they can with the public on the other hand. There is also the need to protect the public from defective goods, unfair advertising, and unfair credit agreements. Thus we have the Sale of Goods Act, the Consumer Protection Act and the Unsolicited Goods and Services Act to name a few.

0-595-32428-2